A Monograph

Making Time for Quality

How to Delegate Responsibility While Retaining Accountability

Harold S. Haller, Ph.D.

ISBN 1-893796-00-0

Foreword

I began to address the subject of **Making Time for Quality** as I was flying from Cleveland to Los Angeles in 1990. The first product of my endeavor was a very complicated picture which you will see on page 61. But please don't turn to this page quite yet because it will probably discourage you from reading
further. I assure you, though, that my approach for finding the time to devote to improving whatever enterprise you are involved in is logical and workable. In order to help you apply what you have learned, at the end of every chapter I have provided some space for notes. Use this space to write down how you will use what you have read to **Make Time for Quality** in your work. I wish you all the best in your quest.

Harold S. Haller
15 February 1993

Acknowledgments

I would like to thank Cathi Bruhn for her efforts to edit the first manuscript which I drafted in 1992. With her help, a paper was produced which went a long way toward explaining how to delegate responsibility while retaining accountability. I am grateful to Professor Howard Gitlow, Bill Vancelette, Rex Kenyon, and Dave O'Reilly for their comments and suggestions which greatly influenced this work. Gail Haller, my wife, provided valuable suggestions to the final drafting of the monograph. All of the manuscript preparation was done by Carole Halter, Lynne Knoll, and Donna Nugent. Thanks for working with me on this project. A special note of thanks to Katie Haller, my daughter, for helping me with the meaning of a contract.

Harold Haller

Making Time for Quality

Table of Contents

Chapter 1

Time goes, you say? Ah no!
Alas, Time stays, we go.
*Austin Dobson ,**The Paradox of Time***

Introduction

Background

The idea behind this monograph came to me as a way to correct a situation I observed during my work with an American petroleum company. At one of this company's refineries, employees attempted to take control of their jobs without the benefit of "profound knowledge," [1] i.e. without any knowledge that allows reasonably accurate predictions of future events. You might be thinking, "How could that happen?" Or even, "Is that so bad?" Let me explain how this situation came about, and then you be the judge.

In 1990, the top executives of the refinery created a *Vision* for their organization which required a transformation in the style of management. No longer were the managers and supervisors to sit in their offices and at meetings directing activities. Rather, all levels of supervisory personnel were to spend their time in the "field" coaching and counseling direct reports as well as leading quality and productivity improvement projects within their departments and within the refinery. Each supervisor's direct reports would make hour-to-hour and day-to-day decisions related to the conduct of business. Thus, the refinery's top executives were telling all supervisory personnel, **"Make Time for Quality!"**

These new directives demanded a tremendous change in the refinery's culture which had evolved over the years to be one of "Kick ass and take names" as the Maintenance Manager described it to me. The style of management had become one which was highly confrontational and authoritative. From the general manager down to the first line supervisors, being tough and rough seemed to be highly regarded throughout this petroleum company. The proposed transformation, therefore, was monumental in the sense of the demands which would be placed on all levels of supervisory personnel. A management style which appeared to have served the company well was being abandoned.

A Roll-Out Process

One portion of the "Roll-out" of this transformation to the employees of the refinery was the decision to assemble teams of "willing workers" [2] to define jobs for shift employees. Called the "Worker of the 90's Project," these groups held off-site meetings to plan their strategy. I attended one of the early meetings and learned that the company had recently accepted an employee proposal which would permit represented workers to be "empowered" to execute all assignments without supervisory intervention. Essentially, first line supervisors would *not* be involved in directing the "routine" activities of workers. Like the television commercial's Maytag repairman, in the future, supervisors would sit in their offices and wait to be summoned into the field to help "get out the wash."

Predictably, the consequence of this decision to empower workers to "run the show" was disastrous. Effective first-line supervisors who were good leaders became frustrated when they were told by shift workers, "Go back to your office, we are empowered." Morale plummeted among these supervisors, while weak or ineffective supervisors heaved a sigh of relief since, for the first time, they were off the hook. Now, an ineffective supervisor could blame the "empowered" shift workers if the performance of the product or process was poor. The grand goals of worker empowerment and improved productivity were unobtainable at the refinery.

Empowerment at Home

A more personal example of the problem of worker empowerment to **Make Time** for other activities is encountered by all parents whose teenager has recently received a driver's license. If you are the parent, and you give your car keys to your teenage daughter or son to run an errand, you have empowered your child by giving her or him "authority or legal power" [3] to drive. Like the first line supervisor, you can only sit at home and wait to be summoned to the garage, police station or hospital if help is required. "The parent," as my father used to say, "must sweat it out." It is up to the teenager to carry out the task of driving the car and completing the errand according to agreed to standards.

Accountability and Responsibility

"Accountability" and "responsibility" are two words that are often used interchangeably when people talk about empowerment. Using the teenage driver example, let's examine the difference between these terms. When the sixteen-year-old girl or boy is asked to take the car and run the errand, who is **responsible** for executing the assignment and who is **accountable** for the outcome of executing the assignment? Legally and morally, the parent is accountable but the teenager is responsible! If the teenager has an auto accident, it is the parent who must rectify the situation — as Harry Truman said, "The buck stops here." The teenage driver, on the other hand, is responsible for acting as taught by her or his parents.

According to *Webster's Ninth New Collegiate Dictionary*, "accountability" suggests, "imminence of retribution for unfulfilled trust or violated obligation," while responsibility is defined as "holding a special trust duty." Because accountability and responsibility are fundamental concepts relative to empowerment, I have adopted the following axioms in order to explain the concept of empowerment as a way to **Make Time for Quality**.

Axiom 1
When a person gives others the authority or legal power to act, the giver is **accountable** for the results of the action.

Axiom 2
When a person accepts the authority or legal power to act, the person is **responsible** for acting in the agreed to manner.

At this point, particularly if you are in a supervisory role, empowerment may not sound appealing. The key is to look beyond the conceptual nature of empowerment and operationally define this concept. Operational definitions[4] provide us with the basis for conducting all activities, whether we are doing business, living together, or even co-existing on this planet. I intend to offer you a concrete definition of empowerment that will enable supervisors and their direct and indirect reports to reduce the natural stress and anxiety levels that accompany any delegation of responsibility. After all, the real purpose of empowerment is to build "a culture in which people take responsibility for themselves and the organization."[5] In creating such a culture "dependency, blaming other groups, taking the safe path, seeking control for its own sake, and self-serving are all minimized."[5]

"What's in It for Me?"

Empowerment certainly sounds like a noble suggestion for some people, you might think. But why empower anyone at all? Because, as Michele Darling's "A New Vision of Leadership" stated:

> "All of these changes reflect the new realities that large corporations face. One person can no longer effectively control a large multi-faceted corporate enterprise. I don't care how many hours a leader works, how much management by walking around the leader may do, how intelligent or financially adept the person is. It is simply impossible to pull all the strands together on one desk."

So, "If I do delegate more responsibility, what's in it for me?" as Phil Crosby used to say. Empowerment does have a number of direct and indirect benefits for you.

One direct benefit of the empowerment process is time. You'll have more time to devote to improving the total quality of the business. Over the years, I've heard managers complain frequently that they do not have the time for quality. Empowering others to be responsible for activities previously controlled by managers frees up the manager's time for steering process improvement projects; working with customers and suppliers to understand their needs in order to clarify requirements; coaching and counseling their direct reports, an essential aspect of good quality leadership; and developing strategies and tactics for achieving the aim of the organization.

Another benefit to empowerment is that decision-making can be pushed down to lower levels. In turn, enabling those who act to do so "just-in-time," eliminates the need to wait around for the boss to make the decision. If you are the boss, this enables you to use your time more efficiently and productively. Clearly, this is a win-win benefit.

Finally, the empowerment process allows workers to take pride in their workmanship. This provides a framework for continual improvement on a daily basis without the risk of tampering with the process, an action which actually makes matters worse.

When a continual improvement process is put into place, over time, actions to improve the quality of products and services will decrease scrap and rework. Productivity will increase, and costs will go down. When lower costs are passed on to your customers as lower prices, your market share will increase, you will stay in business, and you will provide more and more jobs. This is what Dr. W. Edwards Deming called "The Chain Reaction."[6]

The Challenge

The challenge is to achieve empowerment without jeopardizing quality, productivity or competitive position. Following is a process that can be used by management to empower individuals and work groups to take ownership for tasks or work. These tasks may originally have been done by managers or managers may have supervised others charged with performing these tasks. However starting in the 90's, organizations will have fewer supervisory people. Consequently, managers will rely on subordinates more than ever before to accomplish those tasks independently and without intervention which either supervisors handled previously or directed subordinates to handle. In order for this to occur, managers must be confident their subordinates are adequately prepared to carry out their jobs. Both managers and employees need to educate themselves to look at tasks a new way, otherwise fear flourishes which as Deming[7] points out can terminate the chain reaction. By implementing the empowerment process, all levels of your organization can work together more productively. And you will have time to work on quality, as much as ten to twenty percent of your time! Imagine that.

Empowerment Overview

There are four phases to the empowerment process.

I call Phase One the Contractual Phase because during this phase, the manager and workers agree to a set of standards of behavior, method, and performance for a task that previously belonged to the manager in the sense that she or he did the task or supervised others doing the task. This "contract" is fundamental, and it must be a "win-win" agreement, as has been pointed out by Stephen Covey in his book, *Principle Centered Leadership*.[8] However, I believe that the Contractual Phase is the first phase, not the third stage, as Covey's model suggests.

Phase Two is the Training Phase. Here, all workers to whom the task is entrusted must be trained by a knowledgeable expert, or "master," to do the task. Training is complete when a worker's level of performance reflects a process which has predictable outcomes and meets the standards agreed to in the Contractual Phase.

Phase Three, perhaps the most difficult, is one in which workers practice self-discipline while avoiding the temptation to "check their brains at the door." Both workers and managers must avoid the mistake of viewing standards as cast in stone. As Professor Iisaka[9] commented to me several years ago, "Any standard in Japan which is not improved every six months is not a standard which people use." This view of standards may seem paradoxical, but in reality, it embodies a method of using standardization along with critical examination to identify opportunities for problem solving and breakthrough type improvements. Consequently, I call this third phase, the Self-Discipline Phase.

Phase Four is the Breakthrough Phase. During this phase, workers collaborate, then workers and their manager negotiate to create the next generation of standards for behavior, method, and performance. But the empowerment process doesn't stop here. Once Phase Four is completed, the process circles back, returning to Phase Two, Training, to ensure that everyone involved is equipped to act according to the new agreed to standards. Then and only then can workers be expected to practice and demonstrate self-discipline in the performance of tasks according to the new standards. The following diagram illustrates this process.

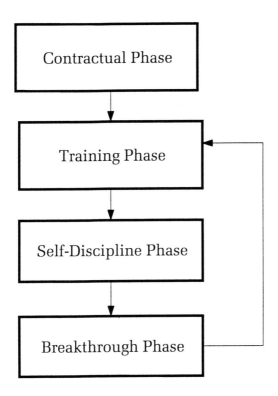

The Empowerment Process

The empowerment process involves various individuals, or players, who fall into three basic categories: managers, workers, and what I call the "point-person(s)." In military terms, the "point man" is the soldier who goes out ahead of the patrol to scout out the dangers and find the best path for the troops. I choose the term "point-person" because it reflects the fact that this individual (or a small group of people) would be responsible for leading the way. Following are some examples of each of the three groups:

	Manager	**Workers**	**Point-Person(s)**
1.	parent	children	child
2.	teacher	students	four students
3.	coach	team	co-captains
4.	executive	entire staff	subgroup of staff members
5.	first line supervisor	shift workers	operator
6.	radiologist	nursing staff	nurse x-ray specialist

An integrated flow chart or block diagram makes it easier to explain the empowerment process.[10] Owners of various process steps will be either the manager, workers, the point-person(s), or some combination of the three. These owners are identified across the top of each chart in **bold face** type. Each person or group owns all the activities under their column heading. Rectangular boxes on the charts indicate activities or tasks; diamonds indicate decision points; and lines and arrows indicate the direction in which the process proceeds. The flow chart contains 12 basic steps, which are encompassed in the four phases.

The Contractual Phase consists of Steps 1 through 4. The Training Phase is comprised of Steps 5 and 12. The Self-Discipline Phase includes Steps 6 and 7. The Breakthrough Phase consists of Steps 8 through 11.

Viewed as an integrated or deployment flow chart the empowerment process looks like the following diagram. Each individual step will be discussed in detail in subsequent chapters.

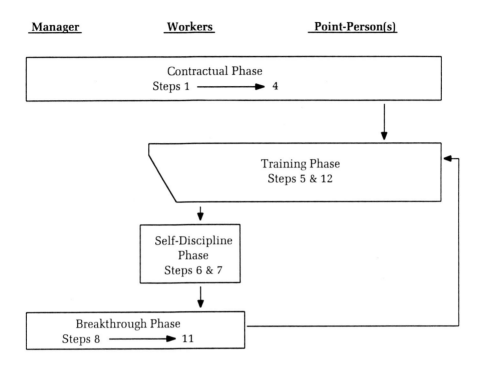

I will begin by describing the Contractual Phase in the next chapter. This is the most difficult phase for managers. It is here that managers feel as if they are losing control of their departments.

Chapter 1

Notes

Chapter 2

*Now therefore come thou, let us
make a covenant, I and thou;*
Genesis 31:44

Contractual Phase

Manager	Workers	Point-Person(s)

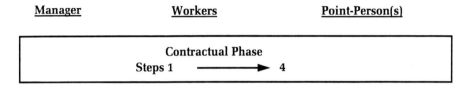

Step 1 ID Tasks for Point-Person(s) to Address.
See Step 1, Fig. 1

Figure 1

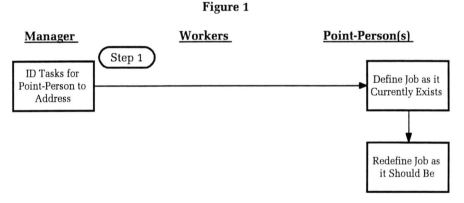

The line and arrows moving from the Manager column to the Point- Person(s) column indicate the initial step in the transfer of responsibility. Remember, accountability always resides in the manager. In the empowerment process, one can transfer only responsibility — not accountability!

First, the manager must identify tasks that can be transferred to others who can complete them with little or no supervisory input. "Since managers often have a different view of

workers' capabilities than the workers themselves, if the identification of tasks that can be transferred to workers is done in
collaboration with workers, the manager can get buy-in right
away with enthusiasm and a sense of responsibility that goes
along with it. The new responsibilities will not be un-
wanted."[11]

 *Manager, Assignment 1*

Managers should start by examining their
daily planners to identify where they are
actually spending their time. This may
require gathering data on such things as time (hours per day)
spent:

- At meetings.
- Preparing for meetings.
- Writing reports.
- On the telephone.
- Supervising in the field.
- Coaching in the office.
- Training (formal).
- Reading mail.
- Answering mail.
- Other activities.

A log sheet is often a convenient way to record these data.
However, it is wise to recall the late Ellis Ott's advice on
trouble shooting with respect to this activity, viz.

> "Rule 2. Get some data on the problem; do not
> spend too much time in initial planning."[12]

Gathering data for a month should allow sufficient time for
purposes of identifying the usual and customary assignments

that people are required to perform in their jobs. The time required for special events can be measured during those periods during which they are actually involved. Here is an example.

Example: Where Kevin spends his time.

A supervisory engineer, Kevin, at the Chevron El Segundo refinery used a random sampling device to record his daily activity on the job for a few weeks in order to capture meaningful data on how he spent his time. The results of analyzing this information are shown in the next figure. Clearly Kevin spent too much time at the computer, a job others could do as well or better than he could.

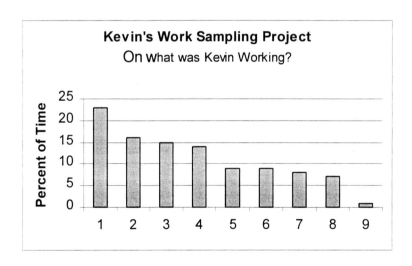

1. Computer
2. Helping Subordinates
3. Other
4. Personal subjects
5. Getting new work

6. Statistical reports
7. Continual improvement
8. Planning
9. Subordinate's issues

Manager, Assignment 2

Second, managers should ask each of their subordinates to perform the same work sampling study to find out, with data, how everyone in the department spends their time. Often these first two assignments flush out non-value added activities which can, by consensus of the group, be discontinued in the future. More importantly, however, as the supervisor identifies what is reasonable and what is unreasonable to delegate to others, the supervisor also identifies the person who can lead the department in the transfer of responsibility while the supervisor retains the accountability.

Manager, Assignment 3

Once the manager has identified tasks that can be suitably transferred to a different owner, these tasks are turned over, with sufficient definition and explanation, to the point-person(s). But note, the point-person(s) will examine the task as it currently exists and consider redefining it as it should, or could be done. As stated before, I have chosen the name point-person(s) to designate the one(s) who will lead the way as the department travels through the tangles associated with the new responsibilities just as a military squad leader selects the person to go "on point" to guide the column and clear the way to the objective.

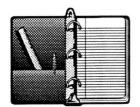 *Manager, Assignment 4*

Because the point-person plays a critical role in deciding how to delegate the task, begin by evaluating the point-person(s) to be selected. It is not necessary that the point-person(s) have supervisory capacities. More importantly, consider asking whether the point-person(s) has:

- Sufficient knowledge of the task.
- Capability to learn the task.
- Interest in the task.
- Sufficient time to study the task.
- Willingness to accept the responsibility to study the task.
- Ownership of a process that is incorporated in the task.

This is a critical decision for the manager. Failure to select the point-person(s) wisely can completely destroy the entire empowerment process. The manager giving up responsibility for a task while retaining accountability will be viewed skeptically by the group of workers who ultimately will be required to practice self-discipline in performance of the task in Phase 3 of the empowerment process. The manager should be prepared to explain the reasons for choosing the point-person(s) to the rest of the involved work group should they inquire into the criteria. This should be viewed by the manager as a sign of interest in the business rather than a challenge to authority.

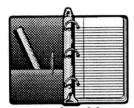

Point-Person (s)
Assignment 1

The point-person(s) will define the task as it currently exists and consider redefining it as it should, or could be done. The point-person(s) should consider the following items when defining and redefining a task:

- The product or output of the task expressed in terms of an operational definition[13] that includes what is expected in the way of quality, cost, delivery, safety, and environmental compliance.
- The general process to be used without reference to specific methods.
- The definition of customers and suppliers.
- The availability of data relative to the operational definitions.

Since much of the above information is unknown or unknowable, the empowerment process should proceed even if clear answers cannot be formulated. The process itself will eventually result in the necessary operational definition of the task.

Step 2 & Step 3 Is Redefinition Acceptable?
See Step 2 & 3, Fig. 2

Figure 2

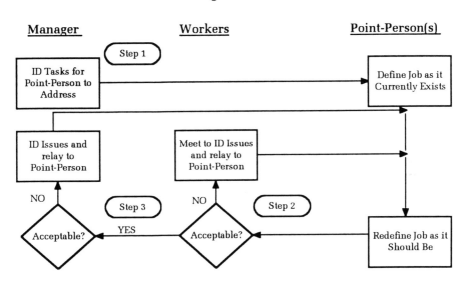

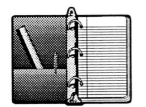

Point-Person (s)
Assignment 2

The "check steps" illustrated above ensure that management and other employees involved in the process will accept the redefinition developed by the point-person(s). This is a critical phase in the empowerment process. The point-person(s) must secure buy-in from other workers who either must perform the job or who must accept the consequences of the job once it is performed. Failure to achieve buy-in results in people demanding their inalienable rights to life, liberty, the pursuit of happiness, and above all, the right to do it their own way!

Step 4 Develop Standards.
See Step 4, Fig. 3

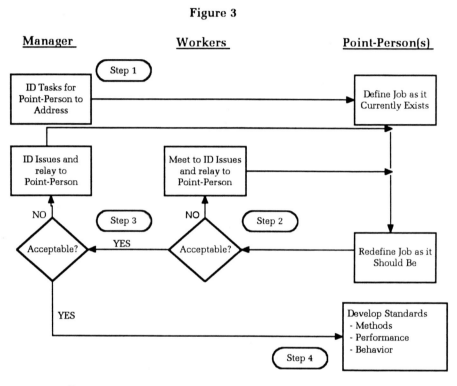

Figure 3

| Manager | Workers | Point-Person(s) |

Step 1 — ID Tasks for Point-Person to Address → Define Job as it Currently Exists

ID Issues and relay to Point-Person — Meet to ID Issues and relay to Point-Person

NO — Step 3 — NO — Step 2

Acceptable? — YES — Acceptable? ← Redefine Job as it Should Be

YES

Develop Standards
- Methods
- Performance
- Behavior

Step 4

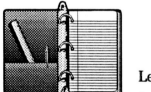

*Point-Person (s)
Assignment 3*

Let's assume that the redefinition of the task is acceptable to both the manager and all involved employees. Next, the point-person(s) develops standards of performance, method, and behavior. Now the question arises, by what means should these standards of method, performance, and behavior be developed? These constitute the point-person's(s') third assignment.

Standards of Method

The easiest but most important of these three activities is to describe detailed methods for executing the task. Usually, a flow chart provides people with step-by-step procedures to be followed. Flow charting enables workers to identify and meet the critical needs of all their customers, both internal and external. Some of the vignettes in Chapters 7 through 16 contain different types of flow charts to describe how tasks are performed. Some examples of tasks that require standards of method are:

- Expense accounts.
- Purchase orders.
- Vacation scheduling.
- Call-out schedules.
- Work request approvals.
- Receiving raw materials.
- Shipping products.
- Project selection.

Flow charting methods are described on pages 60 and 61 in Chapter 5.

Standards of Performance

Typically, performance standards are identified by examining the process flow diagram which describes the standard method for executing the task. Performance issues are identified wherever decision points occur on the flow chart. Performance issues arise any time the activity flow must be interrupted to ask questions such as:

- Customer accepts?
- OK to continue?
- Paperwork available?
- Approvals secured?

Performance standards can be defined and set by management which are not arbitrary numerical goals. When performance standards are set, then the point-person(s) can define performance measures. Based on the manager's directives, the point-person(s) decides what constitutes acceptable standards. Later, in Step 7, workers will review these performance measures in light of agreed to standards in order to decide whether or not there is a gap between the plan and the actual performance. At this stage, decisions about common and special cause variation can be examined. Either the method standard will be retained, or it will be improved by using a structured process improvement approach (for common cause variations) or corrective action (for special cause variations).

Standards of Behavior

The real challenge of Step 4 is to develop standards of behavior relative to the task. To ensure success, I strongly recommend including dialogue in the "Redefine the job as it should be" activity (see Steps 2 and 3) which ensures that both workers and the manager reach consensus about acceptable behaviors while performing the task. What are the behaviors required from both workers and the manager? Just ask the people responsible for doing the work. They will supply the answers. Here are a few good examples.

Examples of Behaviors

- Workers will report all data and events accurately.
- Management will not kill the messenger.
- Workers will not play practical jokes on their co-workers.
- Workers agree to follow the standards unless there is risk to life, the environment, or property.
- When evaluating potential process changes, it is acceptable to abandon a change and report that it did not work.

At this stage, the Contractual Phase is complete, and the participants move on to Phase Two, the Training Phase.

Chapter 2

Assignments

Step 1. Identify Tasks and Point-Person(s).

Step 4. Develop Standards for One Task Identified above.

Chapter 3

Knowledge is power.
*Hobbes, **Leviathan***

Training Phase

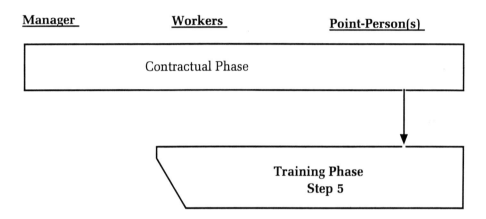

Step 5 Develop and Provide Training.
See Step 5, Fig. 4

Once the standards of method, performance and behavior have been established, the next step is to provide the training for all workers involved in the task. Workers cannot be empowered unless training, if and when needed, has been developed, delivered, and successfully completed.

Undue variation in performance occurs when one worker is left to learn from another worker, usually the last to have learned the job. This worker-training-worker syndrome, which Deming refers to as an example of Rule 4 of the "Experiment with the Funnel,"[14] can be avoided by following four principles of training.

Principle 1. All training should be done by a "master." The master is not a hack,[15] one who thinks he knows it all, but rather one who has profound knowledge about the process. The master is the one who understands the theory as well as the method, the "whys" as well as the "hows." The master can come from any level of the organization. This person need not be either the manager or a member of the point-person's(s') team. The master enjoys transferring to others all her or his knowledge about the task in question and the standards of method and performance defined and developed by the point-person(s).

Principle 2. Training of workers must be provided "just-in-time." Provide all training as needed. Avoid long delays between training and the real-world opportunity to put into practice what was learned. Often, by the time workers have a chance to apply what they have learned, several days, weeks, or even months have passed. There is no way the workers can test out the standards of method and behavior, nor is there a way to assess the effectiveness of the redefined task. Consequently, workers are forced to "get the wash out" by relying on their creative bent or ingenuity. "Stamping out fires," becomes the way to accomplish things.

Principle 3. Train workers to do the job using their own language. Always use everyday language when you train. Never try to teach new subject matter and a new language at the same time. Convert jargon and unfamiliar terms into language the workers will understand. This accelerates learning and reduces confusion.

Principle 4. People learn in different ways. As personality studies have shown, people learn in different ways. Some of these ways include:

- Looking at pictures.
- Hands-on-practice.
- Learning about theory.
- Following step-by-step procedures.
- Reading instructions or explanations.
- Listening and watching audio-visual presentations.

Ideally, the master will train the workers, by doing the task with them, studying how they do it, and then letting them act on their own.

The master "studies" the training by observing the trainees performing the task. Then the master describes to the trainees what was observed. Effective communication includes both praise for what is being done correctly and suggestions for improvement. Feedback from just-in-time training should be gathered and used in two ways:

1.   To revise the general body of knowledge and training offered with the aim toward continual improvement.

2.   To provide additional training in alternate forms to meet the specific needs of people already exposed to just-in-time training.

Referring to Figure 4, assuming training is necessary (which is the conclusion of almost every empowerment case study to date), do not go beyond Step 5 until the "Training Complete?" question can be answered with a "Yes!"

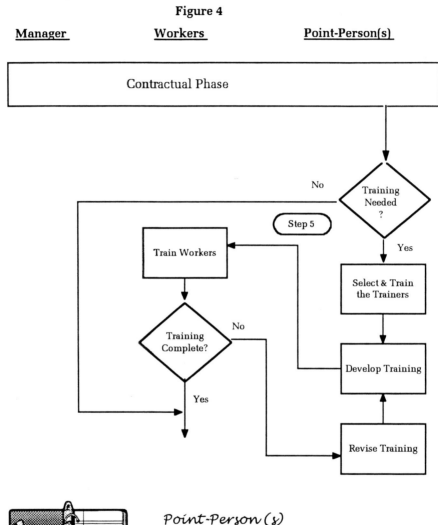

Figure 4

| Manager | Workers | Point-Person(s) |

Note that the training phase involves both workers and point-person(s) but not managers. The workers are the people receiving the training while the point-person(s) select the trainer(s), help develop the training material, may help or lead the training, and certify workers' competence relative to the task.

By what method can the point-person(s) working with the trainer(s) certify that worker training is complete? Final exams usually assess the effectiveness of the trainer and training methods, but exams provide no information about how much has been learned. Observation in the field is required as a follow-up to training. Observation enables someone to determine whether training is complete. The observer should be the trainer or some other qualified person who understands the standards of method, performance, and behavior. The observer could be the manager if appropriate.

The fact that the manager does not play an active role in the Training Phase enables the manager to find time to work on quality related issues. This is time the manager can spend:

- leading improvement teams
- reviewing the progress of improvement teams
- sponsoring improvement teams
- working with customers to understand their issues
- helping suppliers to understand their customers' issues.

Chapter 3

Assignment

Step 5. List Training Needs.

_____

_____

_____

_____

_____

_____

_____

_____

_____

Chapter 4

Our behaviors are all we have to satisfy our needs.
William Glasser, M.D., **Control Theory**

Self-Discipline Phase

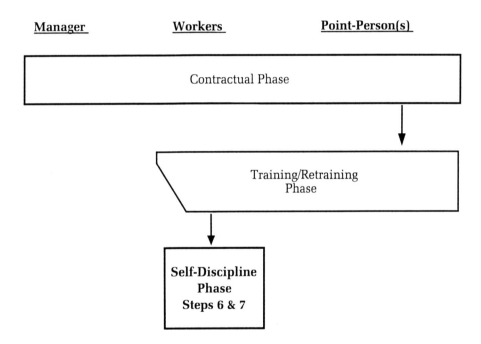

Manager   **Workers**   **Point-Person(s)**

Contractual Phase

Training/Retraining
Phase

**Self-Discipline
Phase
Steps 6 & 7**

Note that the managers and point-person(s) are not involved in this phase of the empowerment process. This is by design to enable them to focus more time on other quality related issues. They will not re-enter the process until the workers conclude that performance standards cannot be met.

Step 6 Practice Self-Discipline
See Step 6, Fig. 5

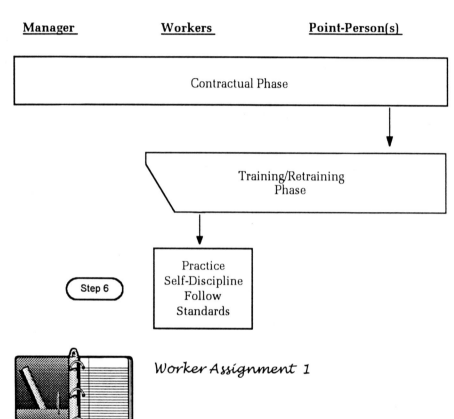

Figure 5

Worker Assignment 1

Only when training is complete can employees or workers be expected to practice self-discipline and adhere to standards of method, performance, and behavior when executing tasks. An unworkable "transfer" of responsibility to workers while the manager still retains accountability can result if the point-person(s) does not achieve both the workers' and the manager's acceptance of the redefined task (Steps 2 and 3) and if there is a failure to develop standards and provide training by a master (Steps 4 and 5).

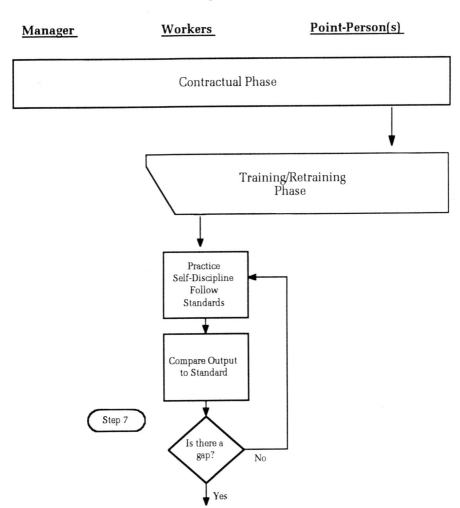

Figure 6

Step 7 Is There a "Gap?"
See Step 7, Fig. 6

Western cultures have rebelled against standardization because many Americans and Europeans believe that standardization prevents innovation and improvement of processes. Nothing could be further from the truth. A study of Japanese manufacturing practices clearly shows you can have both standardization and continual improvement.[16] The key is to have agreed upon standards of performance which are monitored by workers as they practice self-disciplined adherence to standards of method and behavior. Step 7 (Figure 6) simply asks a question, "Is there a gap?" This refers to a gap between the expected and actual performance levels achieved by workers. Statistical methods such as control charts can be used here to determine whether the process is stable and acceptable, stable and unacceptable, or unstable.[16] The latter two cases indicate the presence of gaps. Each case will be discussed in more detail below. Finally, detailed instructions for setting up meaningful control charts are provided.

Suppose the Environmental Protection Agency (EPA) requires that a production process not emit a pollutant to the atmosphere beyond a maximum (MAX) level. The measurement of this pollutant constitutes one appropriate measure of performance in this case. Data are gathered for 28 months to establish whether or not the process is capable of meeting this requirement (not an arbitrary numerical goal).

Case 1. Stable and Acceptable

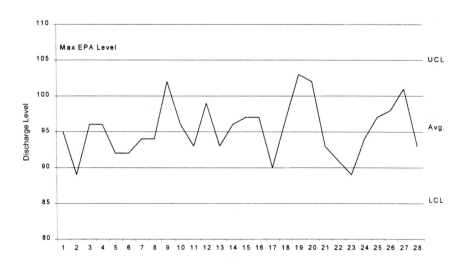

The control chart for Case 1 represents a process that is in a state of statistical control about an average which is sufficiently distant from the goal. This means that despite the variation inherent in the process, the workers can be confident there is little or no chance that the process output will exceed the upper specification limit set by the customer, in this case the EPA. No gap is indicated in this case. Moreover, the concept of being in a state of statistical control means that in the future one would expect this system to remain centered at the indicated average with the same standard deviation equal to (UCL-LCL)/6.

Case 2. Stable and Unacceptable

The control chart below represents a process that is in a state of statistical control about an average. However, either because there is too much inherent variation or because the average is too high, the output of the process will not be suitable for the customer unless the supplier is able to segregate the acceptable from the unacceptable discharge and re-process the unacceptable without incurring undue losses. A gap is indicated here.

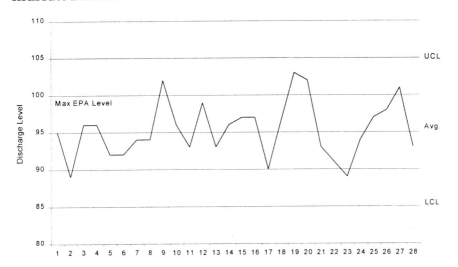

Case 3. Unstable

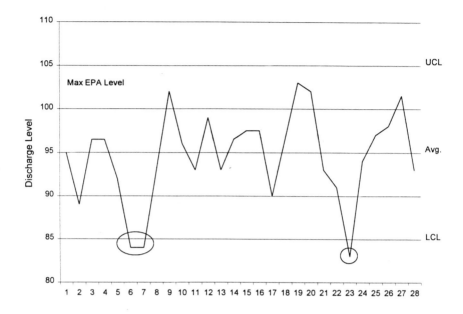

The control chart above depicts an unstable and, therefore, unpredictable process. Even though the instability indicated here by discharge levels below the lower control limit (LCL) reflects improved operations, there is no guarantee that such special causes will not occur on the high side and result in EPA citations for violating discharge limits. Therefore, this is a highly undesirable state. A gap is indicated in this case too. A few examples of factors contributing to the performance measures exceeding the control limits are:

- Raw material variation.
- Failure of workers to adhere to standards of method.
- Natural events.
- Inadequate training.
- Manager intervention.

The A, B, C's of Setting Up and
Analyzing Control Charts

 ### A. Selecting the Right Measurement Scale

Before the point person(s) can set up and analyze control charts, the scales for the performance measures agreed upon in the Contractual Phase must be determined. In practice, there are two types to consider, viz.

1. Categorical scale data
2. Interval scale data.

Categorical scale data occur in cases where there are two possible categories of outcomes for observations, good or bad, in- specification or out-of-specification. For example, suppose the standard of performance requires a sample of n items to be taken from each batch or each hour during a shift. Once the sample has been taken, the number of defective items is counted. The number of defectives, denoted by k, is a categorical scale measurement. The data can be summarized using statistics like:

1. k, the number of defectives in the sample
2. $p = k/n$, the proportion of the sample that is defective,
3. $P = 100 (k/n)$, the percent of the sample that is defective.

Another type of categorical data occurs when the sample of n items is inspected and the number of defects observed on each item is counted. The total number of defects, denoted by C, in this case can be any integer value from zero to infinity.

Most measurements, however, are in the form of interval scale data. Cost, time, volume, labor hours, percent utilization of equipment, weight of shipment, product length, distance traveled, etc. are a few typical examples. Data from this scale will be denoted by X. Some non-typical examples of interval scale data include cases where there is 100 percent inspection of samples and the number of defectives or defects are counted. Here, despite the fact that the data are integer values, they are interval scale data and not categorical data.

 ### B. Selecting the Appropriate Control Chart

Now that the point-person(s) has determined the measurement scale to be used for each standard of performance, the appropriate control chart can be selected and set up. Although there are four possible types of control charts for categorical data, only two need be considered in practice. There is one type of control chart that is most appropriate for interval scale data that is recommended. Thus, three types of control charts will be described, P-charts, C-charts, and X-MR-charts.

P-charts are used when the statistic being analyzed is the percent of defective items in a sample of size n. Since in practice the sample size, n, can vary, the general form of the P-chart will be described. Begin by analyzing m consecutive samples of size n_i which were gathered by the workers based on the standard of behavior agreed upon in the Contractual Phase. Each of these samples is intended to provide a measure of performance which likewise was agreed upon in the Contractual Phase. How large should m be? A good "rule of thumb" for m to satisfy is the following inequality:

$$20 < m < 30.$$

Next, calculate the overall average, un-weighted percent defective based on the following formula:

$$P_{average} = \{\ P_1 + P_2 + \cdots + P_m\ \} \div m$$

where $P_i = 100 \cdot k_i \div n_i$ and k_i is the number of defectives in the sample of size n_i, for $i = 1, 2, \cdots, m$. In this way, undo weight will not be given to those observations from large sample sizes. Using this result, the appropriate measure of variation for the P-chart is the standard deviation which is calculated as follows:

$$S_p = \{\ P_{average} \cdot [\ 100 - P_{average}\ ] \div n_{average}\ \}^{\frac{1}{2}}$$

where $n_{average} = \{\ n_1 + n_2 + \cdots + n_m\ \} \div m$.

Finally, the upper and lower control limits are calculated based on the $P_{average}$ and S_p values obtained above:

$$\text{Upper Control Limit for P (UCL}_p) = P_{average} + 3 \cdot S_p$$

and

$$\text{Lower Control Limit for P (LCL}_p) = P_{average} - 3 \cdot S_p.$$

As a suggestion, in order to determine control limits which are most sensitive to detecting gaps relative to the standard of performance measure, eliminate any P_i from the data set being analyzed which is greater than the upper control limit or less than the lower control limit and repeat the calculations of $P_{average}$ and S_p with the reduced data set. However, one word of caution, do not delete more than 10 percent of the data available for analysis. If this occurs, gather another set of m samples for analysis or consider the process unstable and work on correcting this situation before going forward.

Here is an example of a P-chart for a measure of performance chosen by a point-person working in a health clinic. The data came from a random sample of patients each week, three per day. Patients were asked to answer one question and deposit their un-signed responses in a box. In this way their anonymity was assured in case they had to return for treatment some time in the future. Fear of receiving painful injections can often bias responses. Each week 21 responses (n_i's) were analyzed to determine the number of patients (k_i's) that complained about excessive service time. Overall the data consisted of twenty-two weeks of observations (m = 22).

Health Clinic Service Time Survey
Proportion Complaining about Long Wait
Sample size = 21 patients

Week Number	Percent Complaints
1	9.52
2	19.05
3	4.76
4	14.29
5	23.81
6	66.67
7	61.90
8	14.29
9	4.76
10	4.76
11	23.81
12	14.29
13	42.86
14	80.95
15	14.29
16	4.76
17	23.81
18	14.29
19	23.81
20	4.76
21	33.33
22	14.29

The initial estimate for $P_{average}$ is 23.59% based on all 22 weeks of data. Consequently, the initial estimates of the control limits based on the standard deviation,

$$S_p = \{ 23.59 \cdot (100 - 23.59) \div 21 \}^{\frac{1}{2}} = 9.26\%,$$

are

$$UCL_p = 51.37 \%$$

$$LCL_p = 0 \%$$

Looking at the data from the clinic's survey, the percentage of patients complaining about a long wait for service during weeks 6, 7, and 14 are greater than the upper control limit. In this case, slightly more than 10% of the original data should be discarded as representing special causes of variation for purposes of estimating the control limits in the future. The P-chart for these data is shown below along with the control limits. Note that the lower control limit is set at zero since negative percentages are meaningless.

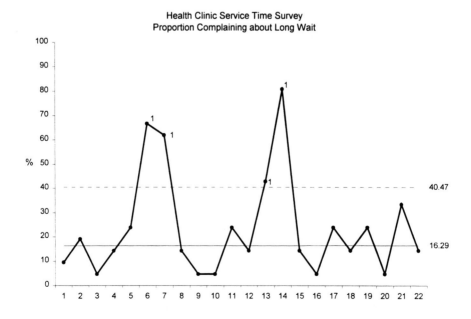

Health Clinic Service Time Survey
Proportion Complaining about Long Wait

C-charts are used when the number of defects observed is being used as the measure of performance relative to some standard agreed to in the Contractual Phase of the empowerment process. Note that each item being inspected can have more than one defect but can be counted as only one defective item. Here the measure of performance is the total number of defects. One can have a defective car which has many defects: paint chips, bad brakes, loose steering, etc. As in the P-chart, it is recommended that twenty to thirty samples be gathered to insure sufficient information is available to estimate the variation of this process. Thus, as before

$$20 < m < 30.$$

Several items can be inspected at each time in the process and grouped into a sampling unit. If possible, the number of items should be held constant. When this is not the case, a modification of the C-chart must be used which is called a U-chart. Since this is a little more general than the C-chart, it will be described here. If the sampling units are the same size (area, volume, number of items, number of days, etc.) the U-chart and the C-chart are identical. Let the number of defects per unit for the m sampling units be denoted by k_i and the size of the sampling units be denoted by n_i where i= 1, 2, $\cdot$ $\cdot$ $\cdot$ m. The number of defects is standardized as follows:

$$U_i = (k_i \div n_i) \cdot n_{average}$$

where $n_{average} = \{ n_1 + n_2 + \cdot \cdot \cdot + n_m \} \div m$. As a first approximation, if the $n_i = n_{average}$ for all i =1, $\cdot$ $\cdot$ $\cdot$, m, the average and standard deviation for these charts are

$$U_{average} = (U_1 + U_2 + \cdots U_m) \div m$$

and

$$S_U = (U_{average})^{1/2}.$$

If the n_i are not approximately equal to $n_{average}$ for all $i=1, \cdots, m$, then the standard deviation becomes

$$S_{Ui} = (U_{average} \cdot n_{average} \div n_i)^{1/2}$$

for each $i=1, \cdots, m$. Finally the control limits for these control charts are

$$UCL_U = U_{average} + 3S_U \text{ or } U_{average} + 3S_{Ui} \text{ if necessary}$$

and

$$LCL_U = U_{average} - 3S_U \text{ or } U_{average} - 3S_{Ui} \text{ if necessary.}$$

As suggested for P-charts, in order to determine control limits which are most sensitive to detecting gaps relative to the standard of performance measure, eliminate any U_i from the data set being analyzed which is greater than the upper control limit or less than the lower control limit and repeat the calculations of $U_{average}$ and S_U with the reduced data set. However, as mentioned before for P-charts, do not delete more than 10 percent of the data available for analysis. If this occurs, gather another set of m samples for analysis or consider the process unstable and work on correcting this situation before going forward.

As an example of a C-chart (or U-chart), consider the following case where the workers (press men) agreed to use the number of defects on three randomly selected printed pages of a newspaper as a measure of print quality. Since the sampling unit was fixed, the C-chart is appropriate for this case. The data are as shown below for samples that are taken each day for about one month:

Newspaper Print Quality Survey
Number of Defects (k) on 3 Randomly Selected Printed Pages
One Sample (Spl) of 3 Pages per Day

Spl	1	2	3	4	5	6	7	8	9	10	11	12
k	3	5	7	2	3	1	4	6	3	9	5	5

Spl	13	14	15	16	17	18	19	20	21	22	23
k	3	7	4	4	6	3	2	0	3	2	0

Spl	24	25	26	27	28	29	30
k	2	1	0	4	3	5	1

The initial estimates of the control limits are based on an average, $U_{average}$, equal to 3.43 defects per three pages of printed newspaper. The control limits are:

$$UCL_U = 8.99 \text{ and } LCL_U = 0.$$

The defects observed on day 10 exceed the upper control limit. Thus, this result is deleted from the data and a new estimate for the average defects per sample, $U_{average}$, is obtained. After all necessary deletions the final estimate of the average, standard deviation, and control limits for the C-chart are as follows:

$$U_{average} = 3.24$$
$$S_U = 1.80$$
$$UCL_U = 8.64$$
$$LCL_U = 0$$

The following control chart plot shows the time trend of the defects per three pages each day. Does this plot suggest anything to you? More will be said about this particular illustration in part "C" of these ABC's.

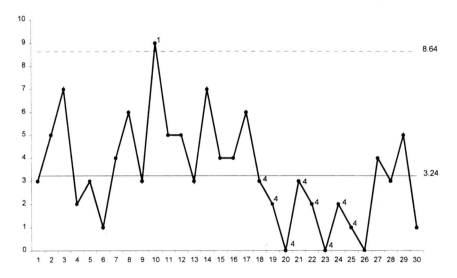

Newspaper Print Quality Survey
Number of Defects on 3 Pages

X-MR-charts are used for interval scale data. As pointed out under "A" of these ABC's, most of the performance measures which are selected by point-person(s) and workers fall into this category. Yield, time, cost, weight, etc. are all good examples of interval scale data. As before, remember that all data should be time ordered so that trends and shifts in the data can be identified. The number of time ordered observations, m, needed to set up the X-MR-charts should also satisfy the inequality:

$$20 < m < 30.$$

With interval scale data the average, $X_{Average}$, is used to estimate the central tendency of the data. The average of the moving ranges, $|X_i - X_{i-1}|$ for i=2, 3, $\cdots$, m, is used to estimate the variation in the process for purposes of detecting control or lack thereof. The equations are as follows:

$$X_{Average} = (X_1 + X_2 + \cdots, X_m) \div m,$$

$$MR_{average} = \sum |X_i - X_{i-1}| \div (m-1).$$

where the sum of the moving ranges is for the (m-1) differences, i=2, 3, $\cdots$, m. Next, the upper control limit for the moving range, UCL_{MR}, must be determined in order to ensure that the estimate for the inherent variation in the system, S_{pcl}, does not include any special causes of variation. This control limit is calculated as follows:

$$UCL_{MR} = 3.268 \cdot MR_{average}.$$

As suggested for P-charts and C-charts, in order to determine
control limits which are most sensitive to detecting gaps relative to the standard of performance measure, eliminate all
moving ranges being analyzed which are greater than the
upper control limit for the moving ranges and repeat the calculations of $MR_{average}$ and the UCL_{MR} with this reduced data set.
However, do not delete more than 10 percent of the moving
ranges available for analysis. If this occurs, gather another set
of m samples for analysis or consider the process unstable and
work on correcting this situation before going forward. In
addition, note that no data used in the calculation of $X_{Average}$ are
deleted at any time! The deletion of moving ranges is recommended to improve the sensitivity in detecting gaps in the
measure of performance agreed to in the Contractual Phase of
the process. Once the final estimate of $MR_{average}$ is available, the
standard deviation used in the X-chart is as follows:

$$S_{pcl} = \text{Final } MR_{average} \div 1.128.$$

Finally the upper and lower control limits for the X's are
calculated using the equations:

$$UCL_X = X_{Average} + 3 \cdot S_{pcl}$$
$$LCL_X = X_{Average} - 3 \cdot S_{pcl}$$

As an example of the calculations for an X-MR-chart,
consider the performance measure selected by a point-person
for monitoring customer satisfaction, viz. "Dollar Value of
Returned Goods." The data are as follows:

Customer Satisfaction

Period	X = Dollar Value of Returned Goods	Moving Range of X's
1	7500	
2	8000	500
3	32500	24500
4	10000	22500
5	35000	25000
6	42500	7500
7	11500	31000
8	12500	1000
9	10000	2500
10	10500	500
11	17500	7000
12	7500	10000
13	23000	15500
14	41000	18000
15	20000	21000
16	11000	9000
17	16500	5500
18	12000	4500
19	9500	2500
20	13600	4100

The MR$_{average}$ and the UCL$_{MR}$ based on the 19 differences in the table above are

$$MR_{average} = \$11,163$$

and

$$UCL_{MR} = \$36,470.$$

After examining the MR's in the above table, no deletions are needed so the process capability standard deviation, S$_{pcl}$, is

$$S_{pcl} = \$9,896.$$

Consequently the upper and lower control limits for the X-chart are:

$$UCL_X = \$17,580 + 3 \cdot (\$9,896) = \$47,269$$

$$LCL_X = \$17,580 - 3 \cdot (\$9,896) = 0.$$

The X-MR control charts are shown below for this performance measure.

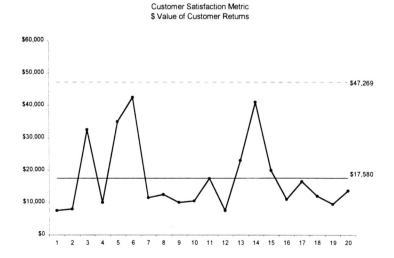

Customer Satisfaction Metric
$ Value of Customer Returns

Moving Range Chart
Customer Satisfaction Metric
$ Value of Customer Returns

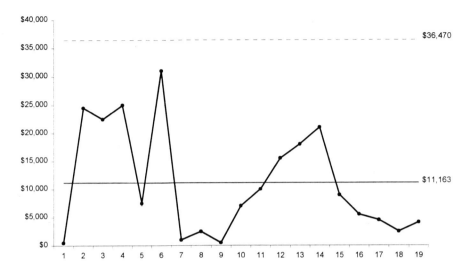

 C. Analyzing Control Charts

The use of three standard deviations above and below the average for the upper and lower control limits for control charts was found by Shewhart to give the best economic balance between under reacting and over reacting to variation in the data for the purpose of identifying gaps or special causes of variation. The rule of identifying a gap only if a single point is outside the control limits can be improved, however, using additional rules which were developed by Western Electric. These so called "Western Electric" rules are particularly useful for detecting subtle trends or shifts in the system being monitored by the workers. Combining Shewhart's rule with the three from Western Electric results in the following list which is recommended for analyzing all three types of control charts discussed here.

Western Electric Rules
for
Detecting Shifts in Control Charts

A "gap" exists for a performance measure if:
1. A measurement is outside one of the three standard deviation limits or control limits.

2. Two out of three consecutive measurements are more than two standard deviations away from the average and the two are on the same side of the average.

3. Four out of five consecutive measurements are more than one standard deviation away from the average and the four are on the same side of the average.

4. Eight consecutive measurements are on the same side of the average.

When a gap has been detected, the average of the points involved in the rule violation provides an estimate of where the process is currently centered as a result of the shift.

Now apply these four rules to the examples in Part "B" above.

1.) In the case of the P-chart, once the Rule # 1 violations are removed, the process is seen to be stable about an average of 16.29% complaints. There were no other rule violations. As a homework assignment, see if you agree.

2.) Looking at the printing errors using the C-chart, it is clear that the process was stable about an average of 4.5 errors per 3 pages until the eighteenth day of the month under study.

Then the error rate decreased to an average of about 2 errors per 3 pages. Here a "Gap" occurred which signals an improvement. The workers are still required to alert management to this change so further analysis can be conducted in the Breakthrough Phase to learn why this change occurred. Only in this way can improvements be sustained rather than becoming simply reasons for celebration. Homework assignment: Using 4.5 as the starting value for $U_{average}$ and $S_U = 1.80$, determine where the process shifts using the Western Electric rules. What is the new average?

3.) The Customer Satisfaction measure illustrates a case where there are no "Gaps" indicated by the standard measure of performance. This indicates the process has not shifted, but it does not indicate that the process is satisfactory. $17,580 of returns may mean that customers are very dissatisfied.

Final Reminder

As pointed out, in Cases 2 and 3 (pages 35 and 36), when there is a "gap," it is not acceptable for workers to acknowledge the "gap" and not initiate action to close the "gap." If there is no "gap," workers are obligated to practice self-discipline and adhere to the standards of methods and behavior. However, if the control chart for the performance measure resembles Case 1 (page 34), but the workers believe there is a better method, this too can elicit a "Yes" at Step 7. Even if the workers are unsure about how to close the "gap," they are accountable for proceeding into the Breakthrough Phase. However, all efforts to close the "gap" must follow an agreed upon process for creating the breakthrough. This is the topic for the next chapter.

Chapter 4

Assignment

Step 7. How will "Gaps" be measured?

_____

_____

_____

_____

What type of measurement scale is used?

_____

_____

_____

Gather about 25 data points and set up a control chart.
Are there gaps?

_____

_____

Chapter 5

No matter how good we become,
we should always want to be better.
*Edward de Bono, **Six Thinking Hats***

Breakthrough Phase

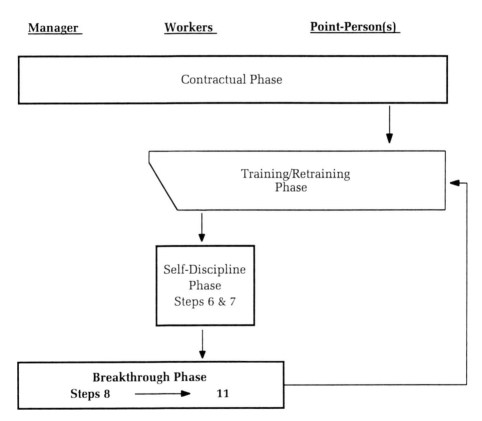

Step 8 Plan a Change.
See Step 8, Fig. 7

Step 7 on page 33 allows all workers to check for gaps. When gaps become unacceptably large, this signals the need for process improvement to begin. This process follows the Shewhart Cycle, also known as the "Plan-Do-Study-Act" Cycle, which is illustrated below. Completing the Shewhart Cycle will take one through Steps 8, 9, 10, and 11 of the empowerment process.

The Shewhart Cycle*

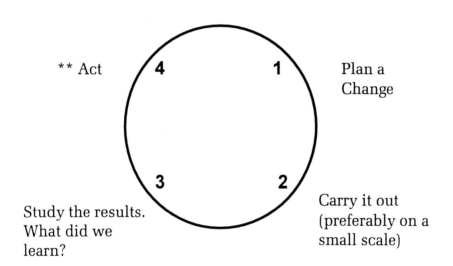

** Act

4   1

Plan a
Change

3   2

Study the results.
What did we
learn?

Carry it out
(preferably on a
small scale)

** Act.
Adopt the change.
Abandon it.
Run through it again, possibly under different environmental conditions.

*Private communication from W.E. Deming

Figure 7

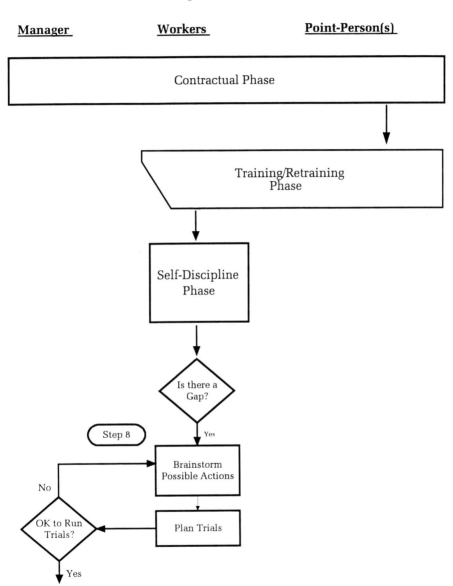

Step 8 represents the "Plan" stage of the Shewhart Cycle. Workers meet to brainstorm possible reasons for the gaps between expected and actual performance measures and to plan some small scale changes or trials. The manager must be involved in any changes to the standards of method, performance, or behavior. The manager must consent to trials pertaining to the task because the manager is the one accountable for the performance. Remember, the workers are responsible only for executing the task. A "No" in response to the request to "Run some trials" only signals the need for more planning. Workers must not take a "No" as a rejection. To avoid this problem, include the manager in the "Brainstorming" and "Planning of Trials" activities. This eliminates delays caused by perceived "Monday morning quarter-backing" on the part of the manager.

Some guidelines for all participants to follow should be agreed upon in order to avoid any negative outcomes from these brainstorming sessions as a result of improper behavior. The suggestions listed below can form the ground rules for improving meeting dynamics:
- Treat all ideas with respect
- Write all ideas on "Post-it®" notes
- Develop a Cause and Effect diagram (see page 63)
- Multi-vote on ideas
- Allow one speaker at a time
- Discourage use of sarcasm
- Provide team members with an agenda before the meeting
- Develop an agenda for the next meeting at the end of the prior meeting.

Two of the outcomes of this planning session should include a clear statement of the problem as well as an operational definition of the customer requirements. The statement of the problem should follow directly from the gap detected at Step 7 on page 33. The customer requirements, whether from internal or external customers, may require some further quantification using the "goodness" concept as described next.

How are customer requirements quantified and prioritized? The "goodness" concept is a simple but effective method toward this end. To accomplish the task, meet face to face with customers and sketch how their perceptions of value or goodness change as a property or service measure changes. Develop one sketch per property. Start by asking the customer for the specification range and the target which is placed on the x-axis. Scale the y-axis using a convenient range like zero to ten. Then ask the customer to indicate the goodness or value associated with various values of a property selected on the x-axis. Finally, by connecting the dots the goodness curve is developed. Some examples of goodness curves are shown below. The figure on the top left indicates decreasing value as the property increases. The top right and lower left sketches indicate the goodness values associated with achieving a target value. Note that the loss in value is not symmetric in both cases. Finally, the sketch on the lower right indicates a case where the higher a property becomes the greater its value.

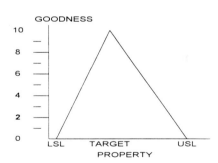

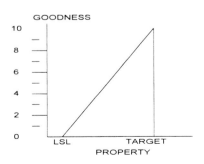

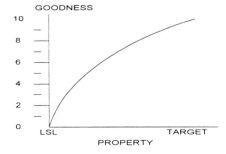

During this planning session it also helps to review the standards of method developed during the Contractual Phase. Perhaps the easiest way to do this is using a flow chart in order to describe the process. It also helps when looking for the cause of a process problem to be able to think about and talk with others about the process. Making a flow diagram which represents the process does not have the limitations of the spoken or written language. Thus the flow chart helps to clarify the process operation. If a flow chart of the process were not developed during the Contractual or Training Phases, one can be developed during the Breakthrough Phase following the outline here.

The "How to" part for developing a flow chart is quite simple. There are really only two conventional symbols which are used although more could be used, viz.

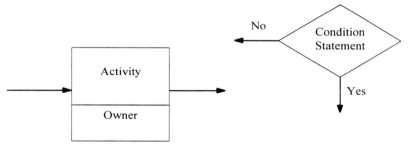

Each step in the process is defined as either being an activity or a decision or condition statement. The steps are connected by lines to indicate the flow of information, material, or, in general, any activity. Each activity usually has an owner who is responsible for this activity. This person could be shown on the activity box as a clerk, manager, supervisor, etc. Every activity has inputs and outputs.

It also helps to establish process boundaries, i.e. where are the start and finish. Both customers and suppliers can be indicated on the flow chart. For each input begin by asking:
1) Who receives the input?
2) What is the first thing done with it?

Then, for each activity determine:
>   1) What is produced by this activity?
>   2) Who receives the output?
>   3) What happens next?

When these questions were asked relative to a purchase requisition system, here is a flow chart that described how the system actually operated:

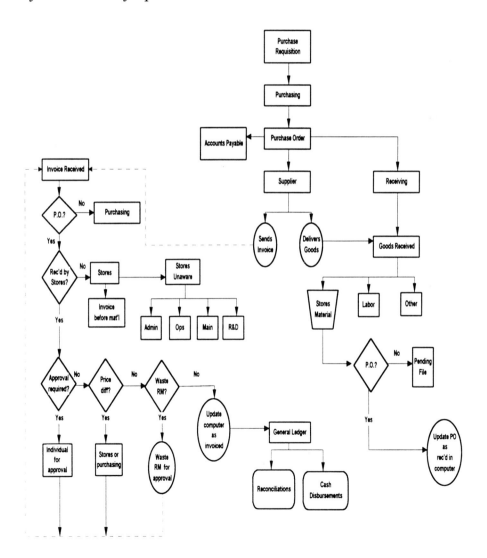

Once a flow chart is generated for the existing process, the following check list may help simplify or improve the process:

_____   Is the activity needed? Does it add value?
_____   Is the activity performed to accommodate errors; rework?
_____   Is the activity performed to undo the work of some one else?
_____   What are the obvious redundancies?
_____   Should someone else perform the activity? Should the activity be combined with other activities?
_____   Can steps be run in parallel rather than series?

In this way, an improved process may be developed. The flow chart below is a revision to the purchase requisition system on page 61:

How the System Should Be Operating

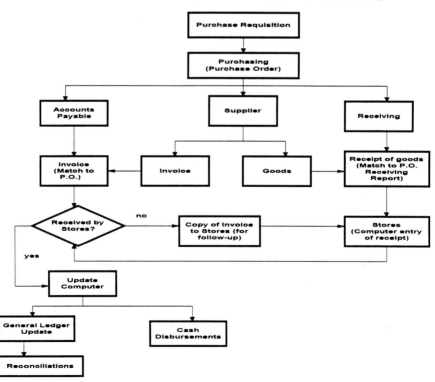

Once the problem has been defined and the process described, the next step is to list potential causes of the gap that is to be studied. Usually this is accomplished in a brainstorming session involving all people familiar with the problem. In these discussions, the group may find it difficult to proceed through the process of identifying potential causes logically. The people involved can easily shoot off on tangents and try to solve the problem rather than list potential causes. Open, non-judgmental discussions must be maintained at all times.

One way to facilitate this discussion is through the use of a Cause and Effect diagram. This diagram generally takes on the following form.

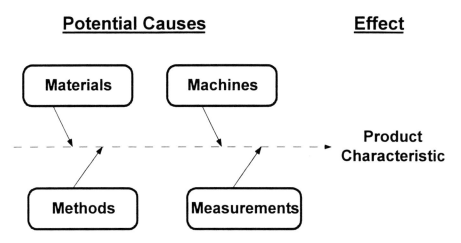

As originally conceived by Dr. Ishikawa, the diagram would be developed as a group of workers brainstormed reasons or potential causes of the problem or gap. During this creative process, while the workers focused their thinking on specific aspects of the problem rather than jumping from one of the four major topics to another, a more complete list of potential causes could be developed. This type of martial arts thinking is more efficient and more effective.

Here is an example of a Cause and Effect Diagram which was developed by a group of clerks working on the gap, "Invoices can't be paid on the day they arrive at the accounts payable desk."

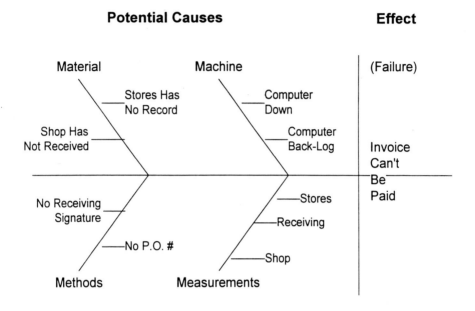

For each potential cause on the Cause and Effect Diagram, the following subjective rating scale can be used to rate the potential causes from the standpoint of frequency, severity, and detectability. The product of these three ratings is called the Failure Mode Analysis Score or FMA Score.

Potential Cause	Rating Scale		
	Low 1	→	High 10
FREQUENCY (F) SEVERITY (S) DETECTABILITY (D)			

FMA Score = F S D

Once the FMA Scores have been calculated for each potential cause on the Cause and Effect Diagram, the potential causes can be prioritized for purposes of further study in the "Do" phase of the PDSA cycle (Step 9). In fact, as one examines the FMA scores, it becomes clear that some potential causes are more likely to cause the observed problem. The clerks working on the preceding example arrived at the following FMA Scores for the potential causes of the gap they had detected in the Self-Discipline Phase.

Potential Cause	FMA Score
1. No record @ stores	50
2. Shop has not received	5
3. No signature	0
4. No P.O. #	10
5. Computer down	1
6. Computer back-log	8

As a result of this analysis, the clerks agreed to examine reasons why the store house had no records of why products were not received.

Figure 8

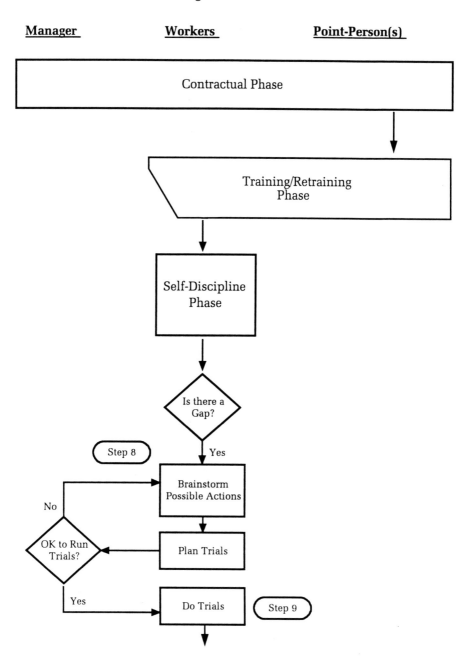

Step 9 Carry Out the Change.
See Step 9, Fig. 8

This is the "Do" stage of the Shewhart Cycle. "Conducting Trials" should always be done, if practical, on a small scale. Both worker and manager involvement is critical to ensure that the planned changes are appropriately executed. Observations— both anticipated and unexpected—must be accurately recorded. The "Do" stage is what the Japanese refer to as "Management by facts, not gut feel." [17] It is important to gather data on the effects and potential causes identified in the FMA that have a high priority of being root causes. All data gathered should be time ordered and graphed in the following control chart format keeping the time scales consistent.

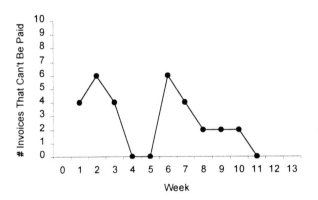

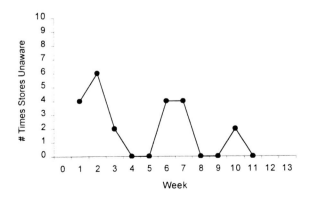

Figure 9

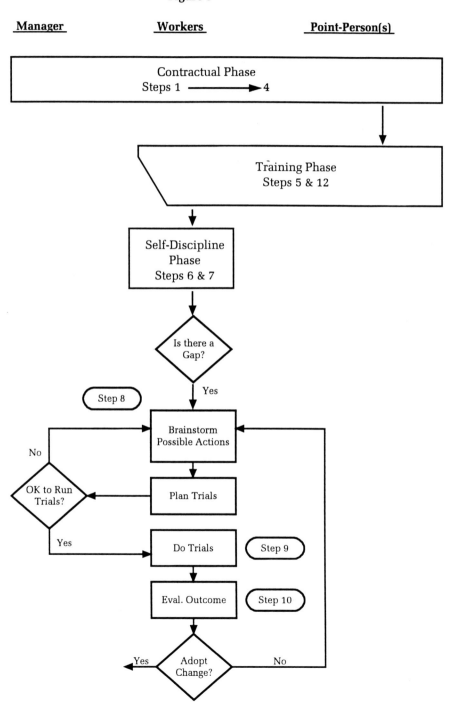

Step 10 Study the Results.
See Step 10, Fig. 9

Once armed with the facts, the workers are ready for the "Study" phase of the Shewhart Cycle. Here, outcomes are evaluated using analytic methods to establish the cause and effect relationships between process variables and performance measures. The objective of Step 10 is to develop profound knowledge of the activity or task in order to be able to predict future behavior. Only then can workers evaluate their options and make recommendations for changes.

This phase is a sequential process. After careful evaluation of outcomes using analytic methods,[18] if no changes can be recommended to the manager, workers return to Step 8, and revise the planned actions. In reality, this is the "Act" stage of the Shewhart Cycle. The first idea or plan did not work, so it is abandoned to permit the workers to try again. The freedom to tear up what has been done and start over should have been explicitly agreed upon when standards of behavior were developed during the Contractual Phase back in Step 4 of the empowerment process. (Refer to the list of Examples of Behaviors on page 23.)

At the "Study Step", the workers must begin by explicitly documenting the variations that exist in the sense of what is and is not true relative to the gap. This is accomplished by answering the following questions:

"What is a gap and what isn't a gap?"
"Where is the gap and where isn't the gap?"
"When is there a gap and when isn't there a gap?"
"Who is and is not involved in the process when there is a gap?"
"To What Extent is and isn't this gap a problem?"

The workers must complete the following table once the answers to these questions are available. The answers are available from the "Planning" and "Doing" stages of the Breakthrough Phase.

Definition of the Gap

5 W'S	DO	
	IS	IS NOT
WHAT		
WHERE		
WHEN		
WHO		
WHAT EXTENT		

Now that the gap has been defined by the workers, they can combine the data gathered from the prioritized potential causes to analyze the variations observed. The top ten potential causes are numbered and listed on the right hand side of the following table which is the right hand side of the table defining the gap. The operative question is which potential causes explain the "Is" and "Is not" for the five W's. Only these qualifying potential causes can become candidates for the

workers to evaluate in recommended follow-up trials. If no
individual potential cause explains all the variations defined
above, then it may be necessary to consider combinations of
potential causes. Further, analytical methods like multiple
correlation, an advanced problem solving tool, may be necessary in some cases.

Analysis of Variations								
5 W's	Gap Def.		Study Phase					
	Is	Is not	Potential Causes					
			1	2	3	4	5	6
What								
Where								
When								
Who								
What Extent								

It is important to note that every potential cause or combination of potential causes that explains all the variations in the
definition of the gap should be verified in a follow-up trial.
The follow-up trial is part of the "Action" step of the PDSA
Cycle.

Figure 10

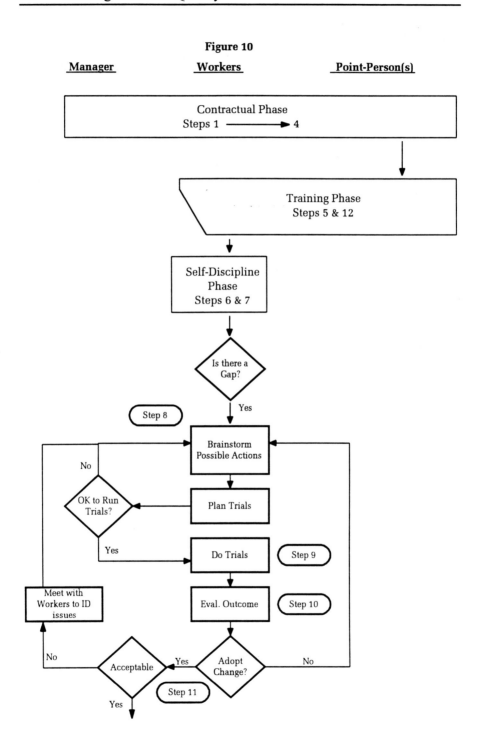

Step 11 Take Action.
See Step 11, Fig. 10

The manager should review the workers' proposal only after workers have agreed to adopt the change as new standards of method or performance. Since the manager is accountable for the task and the results of performing the task, any proposed changes adopted by the workers in Step 10 must be accepted by the manager. Step 11 should never be omitted or circumvented by workers. On the surface, this step may appear to "dis-empower" the workers, but in reality, it provides an orderly basis for affecting change.

After any change to the standards of method, performance or behavior, a process for monitoring the effects of these changes must be initiated. This step, therefore, should include:

- Measurements to be made
- Frequency of measurement
- Criteria for success
- Persons responsible for
    (1) making the measurements
    (2) plotting the results, and
    (3) analyzing the chart for indications of change
- Reporting procedure.

Chapter 5

Notes

_____

_____

_____

_____

_____

_____

_____

_____

_____

_____

_____

Chapter 6

*The most successful corporation of the
1990's will be something called a
learning organization.*
Peter M. Senge, **The Fifth Discipline**

Training Phase (Revisited)

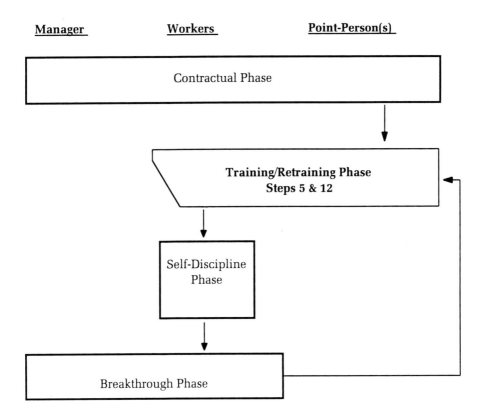

Step 12 Develop and Provide Retraining.
See Step 12, Fig. 11

The final step in the empowerment process ensures that revised training is developed, delivered and successfully completed by all workers involved in the task. Consequently, you return to the "Select Trainer" box in the flowchart. Once all 12 steps are put together, the empowerment process becomes a never ending process.

This "unbroken circle" offers continuing opportunities for developing and practicing standardization, identifying improvement opportunities, and making breakthroughs in how tasks are executed. Over time, the process operationalizes Kano's Quality-in-Daily-Work/Process Improvement Cycle, while paving the way for empowerment of employees.

Kano's Cycles*

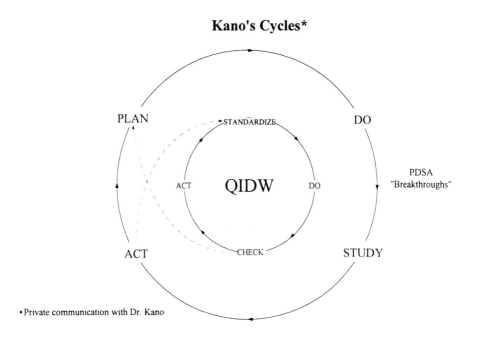

* Private communication with Dr. Kano

Figure 11

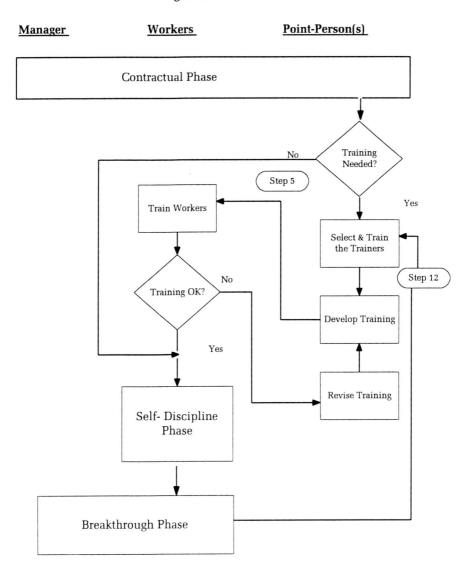

When all 12 steps of the empowerment process are put together, we have an overview of:

How to Make Time for Quality

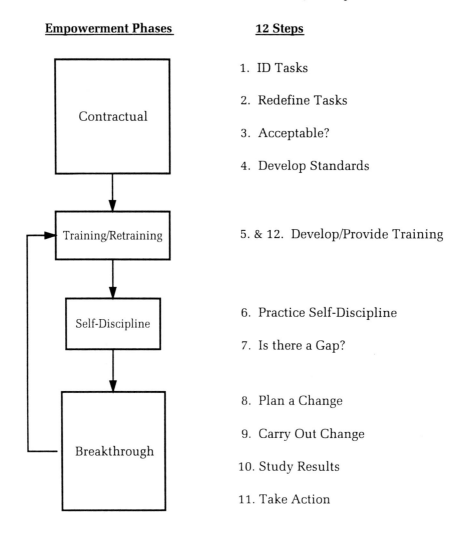

Empowerment Phases

Contractual

Training/Retraining

Self-Discipline

Breakthrough

12 Steps

1. ID Tasks

2. Redefine Tasks

3. Acceptable?

4. Develop Standards

5. & 12. Develop/Provide Training

6. Practice Self-Discipline

7. Is there a Gap?

8. Plan a Change

9. Carry Out Change

10. Study Results

11. Take Action

Figure 12, which follows, illustrates the process as it would appear using the format of an integrated flow chart. The never-ending cycle of steps results in a system of continual improvement that is ideally suited to improve work processes.

Figure 12

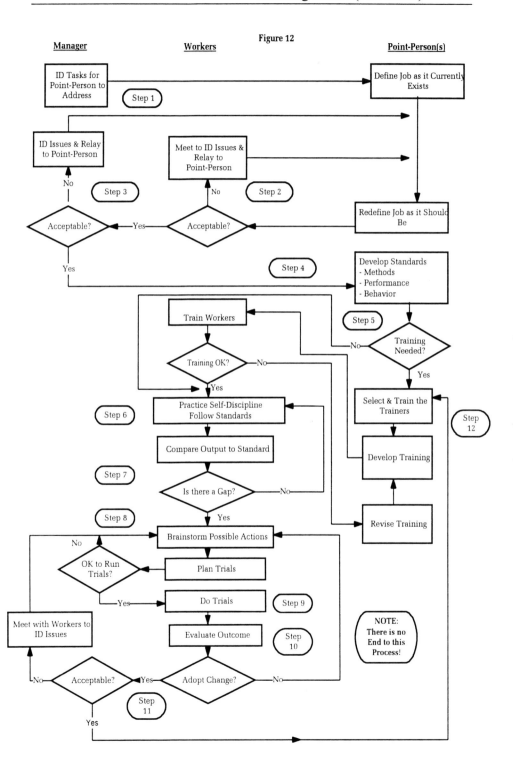

Chapter 6

Notes

_____

_____

_____

_____

_____

_____

_____

_____

_____

_____

Chapter 7

There is nothing better for a man,
than that he should eat and drink,
and that he should make his
soul enjoy good in his labour.
Ecclesiastes 2:24

Making Time for Quality in an Invoice Department

Introduction

This case study began when my client, Linda, and I discussed the need to empower Christie, a clerk in the Invoice Department, to work in a self directed manner. In this way Linda would not have to hover over Christie asking her if there were any problems. Christie would not feel as if she were constantly under surveillance. Linda needed time to focus her attention on both customer and sales representative type issues which were increasing in frequency as the company was expanding rapidly. In fact the president had complained to me that Linda did not have time to monitor Christie's every move.

The Standards of Method

Christie and I began to implement the empowerment process by meeting to discuss the Standards of Method for processing invoices and for order indexing and scanning in her department. Since these were duties taught by Linda, we did not include her in the discussions. The ordinary flow chart shown in Figure 13 described Christie's duties. When we reviewed this with Linda, she agreed it accurately depicted the way invoicing clerks were to perform their duties.

Standards of Performance

We included a box in the flow diagram with dashed lines to indicate an unspecified activity which Christie would perform when there were equipment malfunctions. In order to gather data relative to such events, the form in Table 1 (p.84) would be used to record the date, time, and duration of outages when the scanner wasn't functioning properly.

This same form would also be used by Christie to monitor her performance on the job on a daily basis. Each day she would randomly select an hour when scanning documents and record the type of document being scanned. For the sample hour Christie would count the number of documents not the number of pages scanned. This information was to be recorded and coded with the letter "S" along with any comments about problems encountered during the sampling time. Another hour would be picked at random when Christie was indexing documents. The same information would be recorded, but the code letter "I" would be used to indicate the indexing function was being performed. These data then would be analyzed via control chart logic to determine the capability of Christie's system to do scanning and indexing.

Christie's Standard Methods   **Figure 13**

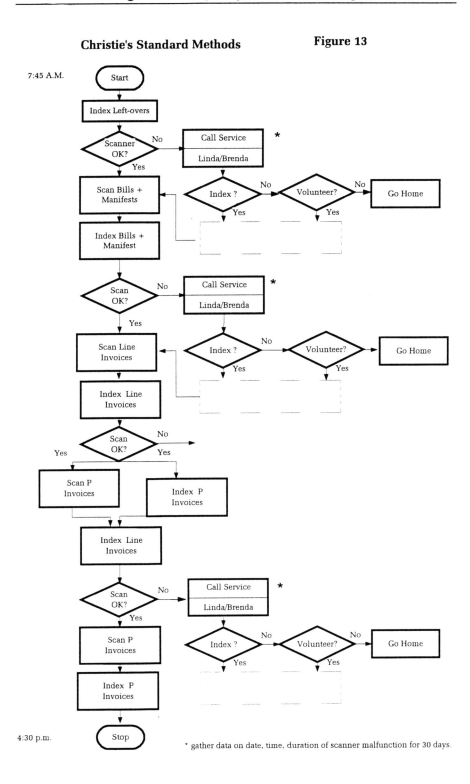

* gather data on date, time, duration of scanner malfunction for 30 days.

Table 1
Performance Standards
Data Collection Forms for Scanning & Indexing Area

Date	Type of Doc *	Activity **	# Doc. Handled	Problems

* Line Invoice	= LI	** Scanning = S
P Invoice	= PI	Indexing = I
P Order	= PO	
Line Order	= LO	

Standards of Behavior

Christie was also asked to write down her Standards of Behavior. My request surprised Linda who had expected to tell Christie how to behave. When Linda reviewed the list, however, she was amazed because it contained every behavior and a few more that she thought were essential for performing the job well. Here is that list.

Christie's Standards of Behavior

a.) Don't get an ulcer worrying about system problems. Identify these problems for management.

b.) Concentrate on the job, don't be a talker.

c.) Adhere to the following work hours:

7:45	Start work
9:45 to 10:00	Break
12:00 to 12:45	Lunch
2:30 to 2:45	Break
4:30	Stop work

d.) Be willing to work overtime if necessary.

e.) Vary the sequence of scanning and indexing to make the job less routine and more interesting.

Results

Once the standards were defined, Christie and Linda both knew what was expected. Linda did not need to hover over Christie. In fact, Christie was given a new private office well removed from where Linda's office was located. The empowerment process now gave Linda time to focus on improving the quality and productivity of the entire department. In particular, Linda was able to focus her attention on the strategic issues facing a company which was growing at the rate of ten to fifteen percent in sales per year.

After about a month of being empowered, however, Christie decided to leave the company. In her exit interview, she revealed that the standards of behavior required for the job, although appropriate, were impossible for her to follow. In particular, it was very difficult for Christie to concentrate on the job for long periods of time. She needed to engage her co-workers in conversation, a practice that annoyed her co-workers because it decreased their productivity. Clearly, from the data gathered, these conversations with co-workers decreased Christie's productivity too. On a positive note, however, Christie found another position with another company which expected her to engage customers in conversation as a way of building a better working relationship with them. At last Christie found joy in her work.

Chapter 7

Assignment

What is the moral of this vignette?

_____

_____

_____

_____

_____

_____

_____

_____

_____

_____

Chapter 8

Power, like a desolating pestilence
Pollutes whate'er it touches.
Shelley, **Queen Mab, III**

Making Time for Quality
for a General Manager

Introduction

This is an interesting case study because it points out the wrong way to **Make Time for Quality** by empowering a direct report, in this case a general manager. The vice-president intended to help his general manager have more time to address strategic issues for his division. It never happened.

The Directive

The VP and General Manager of the Division, Ben, met with his Plant Manager, Dick, in one of their coaching and mentoring sessions. Ben told Dick to empower his National Sales Manager and Sales Representatives to make all decisions about accepting or rejecting sales offers. When I had a chance to meet with Dick and discuss the directive from Ben, I found Dick hostile, anxious, defensive, and, in general, extremely negative about this assignment. In fact, contrary to Ben's directive, Dick had not delegated all responsibility to the Sales Department as the following paragraph from a memo indicates.

Memorandum

"The management of discounts and concessions for national sales is delegated to the Sales Department with the exception of: controls, setting of the annual targets, approval of deviations from our standard terms and conditions, and special circumstances such as our demonstration products."

The Empowerment Process

In our conversations, I tried to point out to Dick the advantages of empowering his sales managers to be responsible for these tasks. In particular this would free up at least ten percent of his time which could be devoted to strategic issues. All of this was to no avail. Dick wasn't interested in giving up the control of these responsibilities. He led me to believe that he did not understand the empowerment process.

In order to help Dick understand the empowerment process and thereby help him to find time for working on strategic issues, I sent him the following memorandum.

Memorandum

To: Dick
From: Harold

After reading your memo from Ben, I put together these two discount procedures (see flow diagrams on pages 92 and 93). A couple of points may be helpful:

> *1.   You need to develop procedures for accepting or rejecting an offer.*

2.   *The A-Co. seems to have too many redundancies relative to accepting and
rejecting offers.*

Call me this afternoon so we can discuss this further.

Harold Haller

When Dick and I spoke on the telephone about my memorandum, I found him to be very defensive about his job. For example, he claimed that there was no procedure for accepting or rejecting offers. In fact to do what he did required a Harvard MBA no less! When I suggested signing his National Sales Manager up for the Harvard advanced management program, he next claimed the process for accepting or rejecting offers required a tremendous amount of intuition.

Finally, I asked Dick straight away, "Would you rather remain accountable and responsible for this task?" To this he simply responded, "Yes!" Again, he reasoned that no one could do the job as well as he could. Thus, since he was to be accountable for the outcomes, he might just as well be responsible too.

It is well to point out that the flow charts, Figures 14 and 15, did little to convince Dick that he could make time for working on more strategic issues by empowering his sales managers to make more of the discount decisions. Logic and reason are no substitute for the fear that comes from the prospect of losing control of one's field of expertise.

Figure 14

A-Co. Product Discounts Procedure

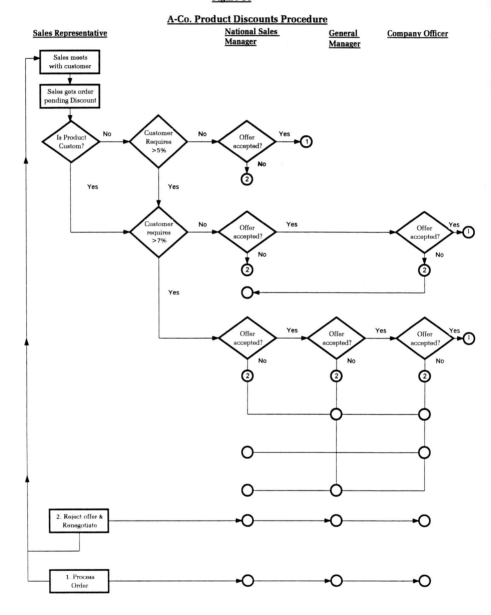

B-Co. **Product Discounts Procedure**   **Figure 15**

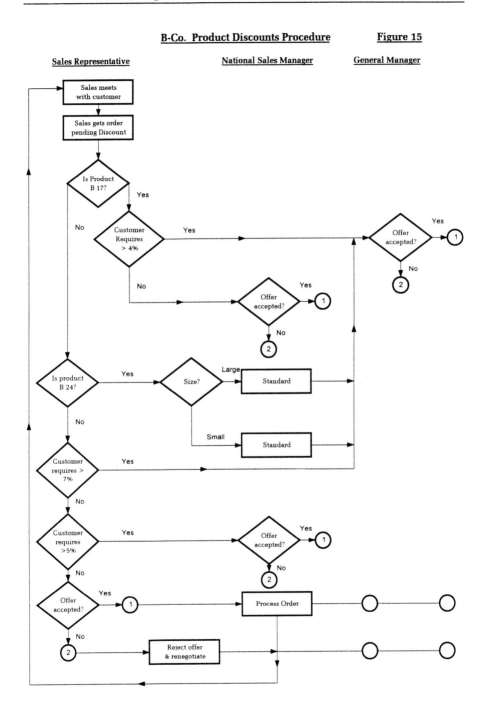

Lessons Learned

What are the lessons to be learned from this case study? Well there are several:

1. The Manager must decide which tasks are to be delegated to his workers not his or her boss.

2. From the company's point of view it is essential that Dick develop the process by which he performs each task whether or not he is actually going to delegate the work. Since Dick subsequently resigned six months after Ben made his request, without ever showing anyone how he accepted or rejected offers, the company in this case study lost much of its expertise.

3. The Manager's boss must work through the empowerment process with his direct report. The best time to do this is during the coaching and mentoring sessions.

4. The company must build a relationship of trust with the managers in which the managers will not be dismissed for sharing their knowledge with others in the empowerment process. Rather this must be viewed as a sign of superior leadership and as worthy of recognition and advancement within the organization.

Chapter 8

Assignment

Discuss alternative strategies for helping Dick to empower the sales force.

_____

_____

_____

_____

_____

_____

_____

_____

_____

Chapter 9

Not enjoyment, and not sorrow,
Is our destined end or way;
But to act, that each tomorrow
Brings us farther than to-day.
Longfellow, A Psalm of Life

Making Time for Quality in Manufacturing

Introduction

This is a case study which began as a project to change a department from a piece-work compensation system to an hourly rate system. One of the major issues concerning management was how to motivate workers to produce products at as high a rate as they did under the old system. In other words, how could they motivate workers without the carrot and the stick?

Standards of Behavior

I began by bringing together the two natural work groups of employees, mechanics and operators, in two separate meetings. Actually, I arranged the sessions like this because I felt that there would be more commonality within these groups which would help facilitate the meetings. Both groups were asked to, "Define the Standards of Behavior which are appropriate for this department." Present at the meetings was the department head. Prior to the meeting I had asked the department head not to participate in the discussion unless asked to do so by the group or by myself. This person had some difficulty with my request but handled it quite well nonetheless. Neither group seemed to be intimidated by the presence of the department head.

The product of these meetings was a list of Standards of Behavior which is attached to this case study. Both the department head and the lead supervisors were very pleasantly surprised at how closely these standards agreed with their own lists which had been prepared separately. If anything, the workers' list was more demanding which was not a surprising result based on my experience with the empowerment process. As you read through the following list of standards of behavior, I believe you will agree that they contain all that a supervisor could reasonably expect.

Standards of Behavior

1. Do a quality job no matter what your job is.
2. Take pride in your job.
3. Eliminate hostility and frustration by controlling your temper.
4. Be a team player; pull together.
5. Practice good working relationships between all team players.
6. Maintain a good attendance record.
7. Have a positive attitude toward your job and all team players.
8. Treat team members as equals.
9. Check raw materials and know their lot numbers.
10. Keep machines and the area around them clean; help keep the entire department clean.
11. Have good communications with team members; maintain honest relations.
12. Don't wait to be asked to do something; use common sense; ask the lead person if in doubt.
13. Behavior must be consistent with all company policies.

14. Abide by all safety rules.
15. Stay at your work station and in your department unless requested by supervisor to do otherwise.
16. Be open to try new ways of meeting customers' needs.
17. Go by seniority on overtime when possible.
18. Be willing and able to trade days with the other shift.
19. Strive for continual improvement on the job.
20. Address high priority jobs as soon as possible-this applies to both operations and maintenance.

Standards of Performance

Next, the groups met to develop Standards of Performance for trainees, individuals, and teams of workers. An average and range type control chart strategy was developed for each operator based on a sample size of two per day. Consequently, it was not necessary to perform any arithmetic calculations in order to maintain the charts.

The operators would randomly sample two skids of product per day and measure how long it took to process each. The number of minutes was compared to standard. The difference was recorded as either "x" minutes greater than the standard or "x" minutes less than the standard. These two results were plotted on the average control chart. The mid-point between the two points was marked with a dot as an indication of the average of the two results. Next, the separation of the two points was measured with a ruler and plotted on the range chart as a point. After two weeks, the supervisors began to meet with the operators to discuss the results of their control charts relative to the need to increase productivity. Samples of these control charts are shown in Figure 16.

Figure 16

Name: *Sara*	Date Hire: *8/26/94*	Personal Daily Productivity Record							Month: *6/95*					
Skid #1	Less		More	More	More	More		More						
Actual t.	30	50	20	20	20	20	30	30	10					
Std. t.	40	50	10	10	5	10	30	20	10					
Time Diff. (Minutes)	10	0	10	10	15	10	0	10	0					
Skid #2		More	More	More	Less		More	More	More					
Actual t.	20	35	20	20	20	20	30	20	20					
Std. t.	20	20	15	10	25	20	25	10	15					
Time Diff. (Minutes)	0	15	5	10	5	0	5	10	5					

More Time Than Standard

Average (Minutes)

Less Time Than Standard

UPWARD SHIFT RECOMMEND TRAINING

Range (Minutes)

1	2	3	4	5	6	7	8	9	10	11	12	13	14
						Day							

Results

What has been the result of applying the empowerment process as a means of eliminating a piece-work type compensation system and replacing it with an hourly pay compensation system? First the supervisors now had time to do more coaching with the operators. However this was not easy. For awhile the lead people just wanted the operators to take responsibility for resolving problems rather than having to work with them daily on quality and productivity issues. Eventually, the vice-president of manufacturing showed the supervisors what was expected of them as coaches. Then improvements in productivity began to appear. The level of rework decreased as the operators learned what was and was not required to meet the customers' requirements. The most noteworthy observation has been that since going to an hourly rate compensation system in the department, a system everybody feels is more equitable, coupled with the empowerment process, productivity and quality have both improved! But, it is important to point out that without leaders that provide the coaching and mentoring for the workers, the empowerment process will fail. Again, Deming was right all along. Leadership must be improved!

Chapter 9

Notes

_____

_____

_____

_____

_____

_____

_____

_____

_____

_____

Chapter 10

The concept is synonymous with the corresponding set of operations.
*P.W. Bridgman, **The Logic of Modern Physics***

Standards of Method Require Operational Definitions

Introduction

A team of workers at a paper mill created a standard method for monitoring the repeatability of the lab's test for the wet strength of news print. The test was called "Wet Tensile." The standard method was described as follows:

Prepare Standard Test Samples

1. Fill a 55 gallon drum with a production sample of pulp.
2. Adjust the consistency of the pulp to 5% and mix the sample thoroughly using a large wooden paddle.
3. After the sample is thoroughly mixed, adjust the consistency level of the pulp in the drum to the production value.
4. Put 100 grams of the pulp slurry into plastic bags.
5. Freeze the sample bags.

Lab Tester Runs Daily Control Tests on Standard Samples

1. Remove a randomly selected frozen sample bag from the freezer each day.
2. Thaw the sample.
3. Adjust the consistency of the sample to the production value.
4. Prepare a "Hand Sheet" following the published PPRIC procedure.
5. Cut the "Hand Sheet" into test specimens based on the published PPRIC standard.

6. Measure the tensile strength of five test specimens and average the results. This average is the "Wet Tensile."
7. Plot the "Wet Tensile" results on a control chart and use control chart rules to detect shifts or lack of stability in the test.

Results

The following control chart was developed by the lab testers. The overall average was 92.6 ounces per inch. The upper and lower control limits were 100.8 and 84.5 ounces per inch, respectively. The point-person, Brian, and the workers consulted with me about the apparent instability of this test as indicated by the numerous control chart rule violations on the graph. (Refer to page 52 for a description of Rules 1 and 2.)

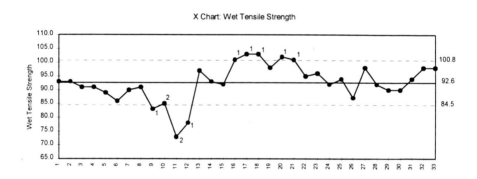

X Chart: Wet Tensile Strength

I agreed with Brian's analysis and stated that these results indicated a gap in the measured performance. "There is a problem with the standard," I claimed. One of the more vocal workers, Roger, questioned my observation. He argued, "We all understand the standard and follow the standard!"

At this point in our discussion, I asked Brian and the rest of the workers to describe the process for sample preparation and testing using a flow chart. Despite the workers' moans and groans, I insisted on going through all the details for the procedure described on page 103.

The method of sample preparation was very clear from the process description given by the workers (see steps 1 to 5 on page 103). Next I turned to the description of the test procedure itself. By this time the workers were getting a bit annoyed with the details of questions I was asking. Consequently, the flow chart for the method of measuring the "Wet Tensile" of samples was as follows:

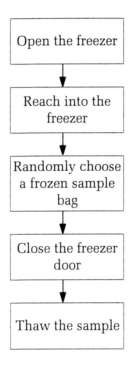

Before the workers could continue describing the process, I asked, "How do you thaw the samples?" To my surprise as well as everyone else, all the workers had a different method for thawing the samples. One person put the sample in boiling water so the pulp was poached. Another tester put the sample in the microwave oven and cooked the sample from the inside to the outside. A third tester put the sample in a hot air oven and baked the sample. Someone else let the sample sit on the drain board of the sink over night to thaw. By morning the sample had started to decay and lose wet strength. Finally, one of the testers put the frozen sample under the hot water tap and thawed it that way. What was needed was an operational definition for the concept at Step 2 of the test procedure, viz. "Thaw the Sample." An operational definition provides a basis for doing business. Without such a definition for the concept of thawing, excessive variation was introduced into the measurement process which rendered the "Wet Tensile" test practically useless.

Action

Once the workers agreed on a method for "Thawing Sample," the control chart for the "Wet Tensile" of the control samples stabilized about an average of 93 ounces per inch with a process standard deviation, S_{pcl}, of 1.5 ounces per inch. The test method now could be used to monitor the test procedure for measuring the strength of the news print pulp. The controls also could be used as a way to certify when new testers were ready to assume the responsibility of monitoring the pulp strength for the paper mill.

Lessons Learned

Two lessons from this vignette are important. The first is the importance of developing controls for any measurement and monitoring the test method using these controls. In this example, without controls most of the variation in "Wet Tensile Strength" would have been attributed to the process, a conclusion which would have led to tampering with the system. The second lesson relates to the use of the flow chart to document the method by which tasks are accomplished. Failure to provide an operational definition of the process can, as in this vignette, lead to excessive variation in outcomes. Although the exercise of describing the process may seem tedious at the time, it is well worth the effort to ensure that all the workers and management reach consensus on how work gets done and by whom. This is a pivotal part of the Contractual Phase in the empowerment process.

Chapter 10

Assignment

Describe the control chart rule violations shown on page 104.

_____

_____

_____

_____

_____

_____

_____

_____

_____

Chapter 11

A government regulation, and likewise an industrial standard, to be enforced, must have operational meaning.
*W. Edwards Deming, **Out of the Crisis***

What Does a Process Standard Look Like?

Introduction

In 1991 a producer of wood chips for the pulp and paper industry was tasked with improving the quality of wood chips for their customer in order to meet an agreed to contractual agreement regarding properties like: Chip Size, Percent Fines, and Percent Bark. Toward this end, a team of workers prepared a Production Process Chart which described the process, the control items, the characteristic of the item being controlled, and the control method. This vignette may serve as an example of the output of the Contractual Phase in the Empowerment process.

Development of Standard

The workers began by agreeing on the process for controlling the wood chip characteristics. A flow chart was used to describe the steps in this process as shown below:

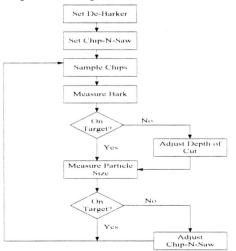

Next, for each stage in the production process, the specific item used to control the process was specified. In more complicated processes, several control items are used at each stage. Which ever is the case, all the control items at each stage of the process must be identified. For the chip production process, this step is as follows:

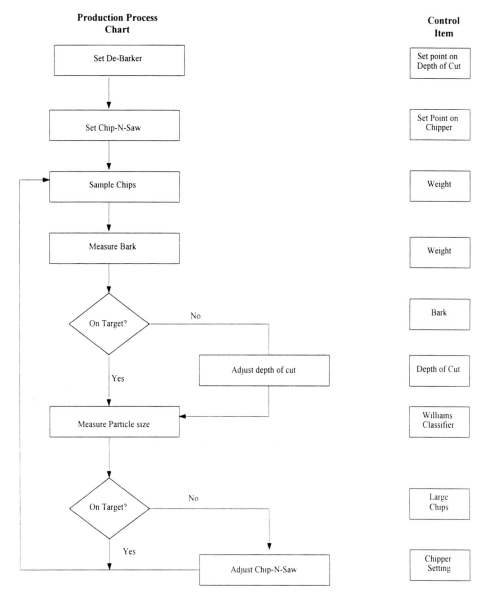

The third step is to indicate the characteristics being controlled at each stage of the process. The characteristics may be quantitative or subjective properties. Later on in this example, it will be expected that the method for measuring each characteristic is available. In all instances, operational definitions are used to avoid the problem encountered in Chapter 10. Here are the characteristics for the wood chip process:

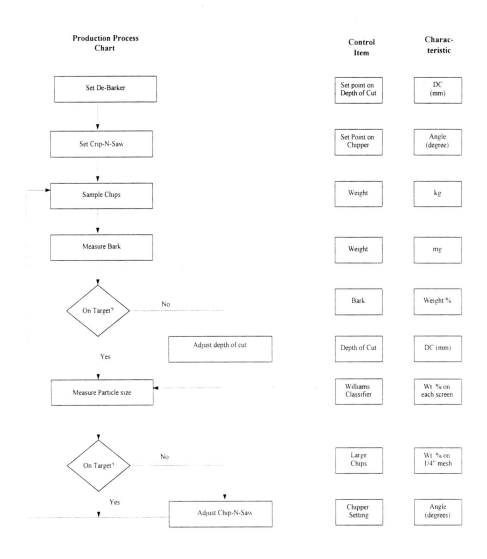

The last step in developing a production process chart is to describe the control method. In particular, who is responsible for each control item, where is the control item located, when is the control item to be monitored for purposes of control, is an instrument used to control the item, what is the description of the control method, and what are the names of individuals qualified to monitor and adjust the control item? For the wood chip process, the detail production process chart is shown below:

Production of Quality Wood Chips

Control Item	Charac-teristic	Control Method					
		Who	Where	When	Instru-ment	Method	Done By
Set Point on Depth of Cut	DC$_o$ (mm)	Shift De-Barker Operator	De-Barker Control Panel	Start of Run	NA	Use as set point last value when shut down until new tools installed by maintenance. Then use standard from control manual.	Sam H. Larry L.
Set Point on Chipper	Angle$_o$ (degree)	Shift Log-Saw Operator	Log-Saw Control Room	Start of Run	NA		Harry L. Roger G. Sue P.
Weight	kg	Lab Operator	Silo Conveyor	12 N 12 M	1 kg Cup	grab	Hong Y. Vince H. John R.
Weight	mg	Lab Operator	Lab	12 N 12 M	Visual	PPRIC 803	Hong Y. Vince H. John R.
Bark	Weight %	Lab Operator	Lab	12 N 12 M	Control Chart	Modified Western Electric Rules - Calc $_\Delta$	Hong Y. Vince H. John R.
Δ Depth-of-Cut	Δ-DC (mm)	Shift De-Barker Operator	De-Barker Control Panel	When Instructed by Lab Foreman	Correl-ation	$\Delta DC=$ k/Δ Bark	John H. Sally W. Lucian S.
Williams Classifier	Wt. % on each screen	Lab Operator	Lab	12 N 12 M	Screen Set 3	PPRIC 934	Hong Y. Vince H. John R.
Large Chips	Wt. % on 1/4" mesh	Lab Operator	Lab	12 N 12 M	Control Chart	Modified Western Electric Rules - Calc Δ	Hong Y. Vince H. John R.
Δ Chipper Setting	Δ-Angle (degrees)	Shift Log-Saw Operator	Log-Saw Control Room	When Instructed by Lab Foreman	Correl-ation	Δ Angle = b/Δ Wt. % on 1/4" Screen	John H. Sally W. Lucian S.

Date Activated: 10/21/88

Revisions: 12/15/88   Approved: John H.
              3/6/89   Lucian S.
              6/19/89   Lucian S.

Note that the date of activation of the standard, the dates for revisions to the standards, and the people approving changes to the standards are indicated on the production process chart. Moreover, all this information is written on a single 8.5 by 11.0 inch piece of paper! This should be the goal.

Lessons Learned

This vignette illustrates several general characteristics about standards. In particular, the standard should include:

1.) A process description.
2.) The key process controls.
3.) The process measurements related to these controls including:
      a.) where samples are to be taken.
      b.) how often samples are to be taken.
      c.) what instrument is to be used for measurements.
      d.) what method of measurement is to be used.
4.) The reference for the test methods used.
5.) The persons responsible and qualified for testing and process control.

Although every standard will not include all these items, it is best to consider this list when critically examining any standard for completeness.

Chapter 11

Notes

_____

_____

_____

_____

_____

_____

_____

_____

_____

_____

_____

Chapter 12

The labourer is worthy of his hire.
New Testament Luke 10:7

Why Can't Maintenance Find the Tools They Need in the Tool Crib?

Introduction

The maintenance superintendent for a Canadian paper mill was disturbed by reports from the millwrights and other trades people that there were no tools available for them in the tool crib when the plant was shut down for repairs and preventative maintenance. Obviously this caused delays in scheduled down time to complete the work plan. Both schedulers and supervisors felt the pressure to get the work done on time but could not improve the productivity of the workers. Finally, the maintenance superintendent recognized the need to empower the workers to develop standards of method, performance, and behavior which would ensure that the necessary work was completed on schedule.

Contractual Phase

The maintenance superintendent selected as point-person, Jimmy Plummer, a supervisor, to develop the standards necessary to get the required maintenance work done according to the schedule. Jimmy was one of the best point-persons with whom I have worked. He worked directly with the millwrights and other trades to develop the standards of performance, method, and behavior. These standards consisted of the following policies:

(1.) All tools would be "Bar-coded" to serve as an identification system for tracking equipment.

(2.) No outside contractor would be permitted to use the tools from the Tool Crib at any time.

(3.) All trades people would be issued ID cards which would be scanned along with the bar-code on the tools to identify the user and the tool being used.

(4.) Over-due reports for tools outstanding would be issued each month by the supervisor of the Tool Crib.

Both the maintenance superintendent and the trades people enthusiastically endorsed the standards developed by the point-person, Jimmy, and his team of workers. Everyone agreed that this would ensure that the equipment needed to do the work would be available when the work was scheduled.

Training Phase

The Training Phase simply consisted of seminars on how to use the scanning device to check out equipment from the Tool Crib. The main point emphasized during the training was that if the scanner didn't work, then the trades people would have to manually sign out the tools. The trainer showed everyone both why and how this must be done.

Self-Discipline Phase

Because the trades people understood that the company wanted them to have the right equipment to do the job, there was absolutely no resistance to following the standards of method, performance, and behavior. The unions totally endorsed these standards too.

Lessons Learned

One of the important lessons learned from this application was how critical the choice of the point-person(s) becomes. Jimmy Plummer was the best I have ever seen. He was able to engage all the workers in the development of the standards, so that in the end, the workers believed the standards were their standards rather than management's standards. In the final analysis, reaching agreements between management and the workers in the Contractual Phase was very easily accomplished. Moreover, this made the Training Phase and the Self-Discipline Phase much easier too. At no time did the more than half-a-dozen different unions ever question the value of this process.

Chapter 12

Assignment

Think about your own work area - office, clinic, mailroom, etc. Why can't people find what they need when they need it? Empower a point-person to develop standards of method, performance, and behavior to improve the system for storage and retrieval.

_____

_____

_____

_____

_____

_____

_____

Chapter 13

What figures are important? What figures should one study by use of a control chart or by any other method? The answer lies in the subject matter assisted by statistical theory.
W. Edwards Deming, **Out of the Crisis**

Customer Satisfaction Standards

Introduction

Customer satisfaction is a concept. Without measures of performance, this concept has no operational meaning. Toward the end of creating a method to monitor customer satisfaction, the senior management team from a distribution company selected a group of six managers to function as point-persons for purposes of creating standards of performance. The six people represented sales, marketing, distribution, purchasing, customer service, and finance. Their mandate was to develop and set up a system to monitor customer satisfaction.

Contractual Phase

The point-persons began their assignment by brain-storming potential metrics for measuring customer satisfaction. It was agreed that each of the six departments represented by the six point-persons would be allowed to request at most five measures of customer satisfaction for their function. In this way, customer satisfaction would be characterized by at most a 30-dimensional space. It was also agreed that the frequency of measurement would be weekly. Each measure would be control charted so that analytic methods could be used to determine whether the metric was getting better, getting worse, or staying the same, i.e. a stable process. Those metrics that indicated significant shifts based on control chart logic would be highlighted on the front of the weekly report much like warning lights on the dashboard of an automobile. The focal point of the report for management would be this dashboard.

The point-persons canvassed the people in their functions in order to get a consensus relative to the five metrics to include in their portion of the report. Thus the Contractual Phase was completed with relative ease. The following list indicates the metrics selected:

Customer Satisfaction Metrics
Abandon Rates for Sales
Abandon Rates for Customer Service
Abandon Rates for Technical Service
Abandon Rates for Financial Services
Inbound Calls to Sales
Inbound Calls to Customer Service
Inbound Calls to Technical Service
Inbound Calls to Financial Services
Average Time Customers Wait to Be Served by Sales
Average Time Customers Wait to Be Served by Customer Service
Average Time Customers Wait to Be Served by Technical Service
Average Time Customers Wait to Be Served by Financial Services
Customer Returns as a Percent of Gross Sales
Customer Refusals as a Percent of Gross Sales
Number of Returns Authorized (RA) for Order Entry Errors
Number of Returns Authorized (RA) for Shipping Errors
Shipping Accuracy
Back Ordered Products
Accuracy of Marketing Promo Material
Up Time for Computing System

On a weekly basis the data from these metrics were control charted and analyzed for shifts. Here is an example showing numerous shifts in the metric:

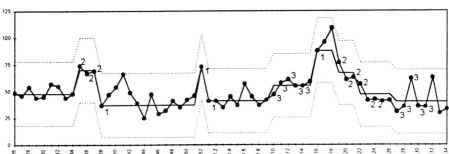

X Chart: AVERAGE TIME (SEC) CUSTOMERS WAIT TO BE SERVED BY CUSTOMER SERVICE

Training Phase

Once the dashboard was developed and the data were gathered on a weekly basis, the point-persons were exposed to the basics of control chart analysis (see pages 37 to 53). Each of the point-persons was responsible for training their departments on the interpretation of the control charts.

Self-Discipline Phase

Each of the point-persons worked with their functional heads to designate a representative who would gather the data for the metrics from their department on a weekly basis and transmit the information to Haller & Company for assembly into the data dashboard. The warning lights on the report summary would serve as the gap analysis which would be reviewed weekly at the gross profit meeting on Monday afternoons. At that time each function would respond to the indicated shifts by explaining the root cause, the corrective action required, the sustaining action required, or why no action was required.

The dashboard for Quarter 3, Week 34 was as follows. The reasons for these shifts are provided during the gross profit meeting each Monday afternoon the week after the report is issued.

Customer Satisfaction Dashboard
Week Ending 8/28/98 (Quarter 3, Week 34)

Special Features on the Dashboard at Quarter 3, Week 34

Dashboard Category/Metric	Special Feature/Comments
1. Abandon Rate %	Average percentage decreased from 12.9% to 9.9% starting with week 30
2. Number of Inbound Calls	Average number increased from 1,916 to 3,906
3. Average Time (sec) Customers Wait to be Served	Average number decreased from 114 sec. to 92.7 sec starting with week 32
4. % of RA's Issued for Sales Order Entry Errors Relative to the # of Orders Shipped Per Week	Average decreased from .0155% to .012% starting with week 32
5. Received & Escalated RA's Pending Resolutions By Customer Service (# of Skids)	Average number decreased from 29.33 skids to 24 skids
6. RA's not Processed Within 48 Hours (# of Skids)	Average number increased from 0 skids to 12 skids starting with week 30
7. % of $ Value of A-SKU's with One Week Stock on Hand	Average percentage decreased from 77.5% to 69.8% starting with week 32
8. % of Products with One Week Stock on Hand (Total SKU's)	Average percentage decreased from 75.1% to 71.5%

Lessons Learned

One of the fundamental lessons learned from this vignette was to gather data, but not too much. It became clear to the point-persons that too many metrics would really just confuse people. Five measures should be a maximum for any department to follow. How many warning lights does your car have? Most cars have four warning lights: low amperage, high temperature, low oil pressure, and low fuel. A suggested method to find the key measures for each function is to ask each department manager to retain those pieces of information which are used frequently to make decisions about customer satisfaction. Keep the critical documents in a separate pile for one month. These documents contain the key measures for the function.

Another lesson learned was the importance of identifying an individual to be responsible for receiving all the data and publishing the dashboard. This person must work with the functional representatives from each department to ensure they transmit their data on a timely basis.

Chapter 13

Assignment

Develop a Business Performance Dashboard for your department, division, or company.

_____

_____

_____

_____

_____

_____

_____

_____

_____

Chapter 14

The wheel that squeaks the loudest
is the one that gets the grease.
Josh Billings, **The Kicker**

Empowering Accounts Payable

Introduction

Rod, the senior vice president of a major chemical company, was concerned about the increasing number of customer complaints about billing. In fact the following Pareto Chart indicates that from 8/15/83 to 1/24/84 there were 54 complaints about billing alone!

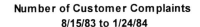
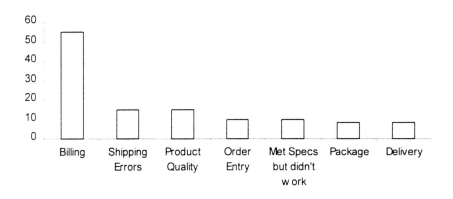

Number of Customer Complaints
8/15/83 to 1/24/84

Because of these billing errors, the average amount of customer invoices unpaid each month was $2,020,000. The accounting department's remedy to this situation was to add more people to the accounts payable department.

Rod, on the other hand, decided to empower the accounting department to develop standards of method, performance, and behavior which would in turn help to reveal the nature of the problem. This vignette describes the outcome of this effort.

Contractual Phase

The point-person in this assignment was Joe. He began the assignment by setting up a meeting with customer service, sales, information service, and accounting representatives to discuss the process from order entry to final shipment to the customer. The product of this meeting was the flow chart shown below:

Pricing Process

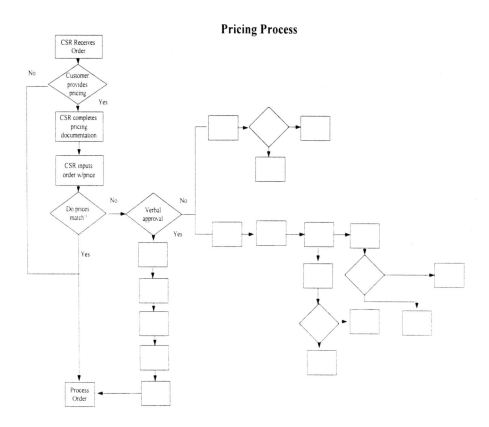

What startled the group as they studied this flow chart was the fact that 90% of the people and steps in the process are required when the response to the query, "Do prices match?" is, "No." The customer service representative at the meeting exclaimed, "How can that happen?" To this question, the point-person, Joe, responded, "We must develop standards of method and behavior for sales, customer service, and information service which ensure that the customer's quoted price and the price in the computer system always match."

Breakthrough

The breakthrough in this process came as the representatives to Joe's meeting discussed what is done as orders are processed. The sales person indicated that frequently special pricing arrangements are made with large volume customers. Of course these deals are approved by the district sales manager, but sometimes the approval lags a few days behind the order which is placed by the customer. The customer service representatives are taught to accept any price from the customer and put it into the computer without questioning the price. But the customer service representatives cannot mark the order price as approved unless the authorization from the district sales manager has arrived at the order entry desk. Joe then asked the accounting person what they did in their audit of the accounts. Rather sheepishly the accountant indicated that if the approval was not marked on the order, they re-entered all prices to "LIST!" At this point you could have heard a pin drop. The sales person was stunned.

Revision to Standard

The revision to the standard that was adopted by this empowered group was the requirement that the auditor must check with the appropriate district sales manager relative to any un-approved price on an order before changing the price to "LIST." This revision to the standard eliminated the billing problem and enabled 90% of the people engaged in the pricing system to be reassigned to more meaningful and productive jobs within the company.

Lessons Learned

There is no substitute for the point-person asking all those workers assigned to a task to meet to describe what they do. Many times this alone reveals the true nature of the problem or the cause of the gap. The process map like the one used in this vignette helps to put all the pieces of the puzzle on the table at the same time so the workers can see if they do in fact fit. The rest is common sense.

The point-person can easily gain consensus when the key players are working together on an issue. One of the aspects of this assignment that Joe did so well was to bring the key players together in the Contractual Phase to describe how the system actually worked and why it had to work that way.

Chapter 14

Assignment

Develop a process map of how invoices are paid within your company. Start with the activity:

```
┌─────────────────────────┐
│      Invoice Arrives     │
│          at the          │
│   Accounts Payable Desk  │
└─────────────────────────┘
```

End with:

```
┌─────────────────────────┐
│                          │
│   Check Sent to Vendor   │
│                          │
└─────────────────────────┘
```

Solicit input from workers that are involved in this system.

_____

_____

_____

_____

_____

Chapter 15

The emphasis on customer satisfaction and processes takes the concept of quality beyond a single production department.
N. Kano, **Continuous Improvement**

Empowering Industry-Specific Teams to Work Directly with Customers

Introduction

To remain competitive in the construction industry, contractors must accelerate the development of attractive features to offer their customers. Unfortunately, these customers for plant expansions, office buildings, and warehouses are not aware of the features that will delight them if made available. Customers have become accustomed to putting up with the features offered by contractors in the past with little or no options for change.

In 1992, the Rudolph/Libbe Companies, a $250,000,000 Toledo, OH based general contractor, mechanical and electrical service provider, and development company changed all that by empowering industry specific teams to work directly with customers. This vignette describes the transformation which occurred.

Contractual Phase

Initially, I was asked by Phil Rudolph, co-founder of the Rudolph/Libbe Companies, to meet and discuss the idea of creating market segmentation teams. These teams would be composed of an industry specific specialist from each of the following departments: estimating, sales, project management, and field supervision. The four team members would be empowered to identify, bid on, negotiate, and execute construction related projects. Phil and I developed an organizational chart based on a model used by Dr. R. J. Wolf[20]. This chart is shown below. Note that each functional department provides the technical expertise for their component of the market segmentation teams, but the teams themselves are empowered to market services, bid jobs, and execute projects for their market segment, viz. food/pharmaceuticals, automotive/industrial, petro-chemical/pulp and paper, and comprehensive regional services.

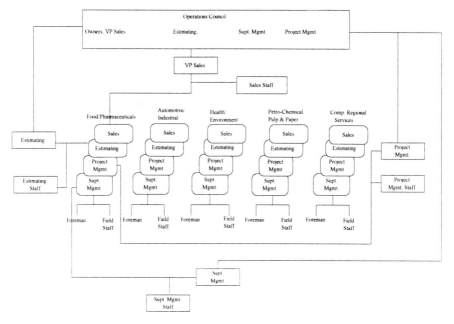

Lessons Learned

The management of the Rudolph/Libbe Companies adopted the market segmentation model because it enabled their industry specialists to identify customers' needs more easily and respond to the changing markets more aggressively and in a more timely manner. This was not an easy transformation, however. Management had been accustomed to making all the business decisions. To make this novel approach work, the senior management from each functional area viz., sales, estimating, project management, and field supervision, needed to mentor their industry specialists. In effect, the senior managers were explaining their standards of method and behavior to the point-persons from their departments for each market segment. What I initially observed was the need for the senior management to actually create these standards. The standards never existed except possibly in someone's head. This should have been done in advance of the transformation.

Chapter 15

Assignment

Adopt this de-centralized organizational structure for your business. Begin by laying out a system similar to that shown on page 132. Indicate the sources of functional expertise. List the services offered by the empowered group.

_____

_____

_____

_____

_____

_____

_____

Chapter 16

People working cooperatively succeed
because a group is greater than the sum
of its parts.
A. Kohn, ***No Contest***

Customer Cooperative Efforts

Introduction
     In 1984 Ashland Chemical's Polyester Division and one
of their customers, a trailer siding manufacturer, had a dis-
agreement over the cause of defects in fabricated panels. The
management of both companies agreed to cooperate rather
than litigate to improve the system. Point-persons from both
companies were assembled in Courthouse Square, OH for a
meeting to understand the current process of making resin and
of fabricating trailer side panels. I was asked to facilitate this
meeting. The point-persons from both companies were empowered to resolve the contentious issue of product defects.

Contractual Phase
     At the meeting in Courthouse Square, OH, the point-
person representing the customer provided us with a plant
tour so both Ashland representatives as well as I could see the
process first hand. I then asked if workers who inspected the
fabricated panels could join the group in discussing the standards of method and behavior. When everyone was assembled,
the workers described their process.

     Essentially, the process consisted of placing on a flat
table, ten 4x8 sheets of plywood such that the eight foot sides
were adjacent to each other. The ten pieces of plywood were
secured together from the top using steel staples, three to a
side. The assembly was coated with polyester resin and the
pre-formed gel coat and fiberglass outer surface was placed on

top of the resin coated plywood. Then a vacuum bag was placed over the entire assembly, secured to the table, and pumped down to a set vacuum level where it was held for 12 hours. After the cure was complete, the vacuum bag was removed so the fabrication could be inspected before installation on the trailer using carriage bolts. It was upon inspection that the workers observed portions of the lamination which had voids below the pre-formed gel coat and fiberglass outer surface. These defects severely weakened the final product. As a result, all defects had to be removed and patched, a time consuming and costly job requiring skilled gel-coat specialists.

Based on the comments from the workers, the standard methods were understood by everyone, training had been provided on the procedure for mixing the resin, and the supervisors had little or no discipline problems with workers failing to adhere to these standards. The Ashland Chemical point-person reviewed the procedures for preparing the polyester resin. One particular point which was reviewed with the workers was the "pot life" of the resin once mixed. Both the supervisors and the workers described how they ensured that the resin was always well within the specifications for application to the plywood substrate.

At this juncture, I concluded that the customer's work force was practicing self-discipline with respect to the standards of method and behavior that had been established. Consequently, I suggested that the empowered group of point-persons and workers begin the Breakthrough Phase of the process.

Breakthrough Phase

When everyone was assembled, I laid out the "Definition of the Gap" portion of the Analysis of Variations form on a flip chart. Then I announced that we would determine what the gap was and wasn't, when there was and wasn't a gap, who was involved with the fabrication process when there was and wasn't a gap, and where gaps did and didn't appear on the panels. As can be seen from the table below, most of the information was relatively straight forward to gather from the participants at the meeting. However, the answer to the following question was more difficult to reveal.

"Where is and isn't the gap?

Definition of the Gap

	DO	
5 W'S	**IS**	**IS NOT**
WHAT	*Voids on panels*	*Other defects*
WHERE	*???????????*	*????????????*
WHEN	*Starting week of 20 October 1984*	*Before 20 October 1984*
WHO	*All shifts*	*All Shifts*
WHAT EXTENT	*2 day delay in shipments, 8 hours of rework, 20 have been found*	*meet shipments, no rework required*

The point-person from the customer's operation needed the input of the workers to provide this information. Everyone seemed to know how much "pain" they had but no idea about the location of the "pain." So, my next questions all were directed towards the workers who actually observed the defects on the fabricated panels.

I began by drawing the following sketch on the flip chart:

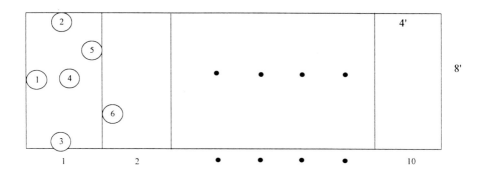

Pointing to each of the circled numbers I asked "How many defects have been observed at location number one?" The answer was "Zero." Next, I asked the same question relative to location number two. Again the answer was "Zero." Continuing in this fashion, I was told by the workers at the customer's plant that they never saw a defect at the positions indicated by circles one through four. Somewhat bewildered, I asked, "Where have you seen the defects?" To everyone's surprise, they indicated that defects occurred on the left of a plywood seam (position five) or the right of a plywood seam (position six), but never crossed a plywood seam. After some quick calculations, I pointed out that if this was a random event on the fabrication, the probability of this occurring was

$$(2/6)^{20} = 2.9 \times 10^{-10} \text{ !}$$

Because this probability was so remote, I suggested that the next fabricated trailer side that had a void be sawed along the plywood seam with the defect so both edges of the plywood could be inspected. The point-persons agreed to this readily because they were empowered by management to improve the system.

Results

When the next defect was detected and the plywood seam opened, the root cause of the problem became clear. Missing plies of wood were soaking up the polyester resin during the vacuum curing process. But why had this become a problem suddenly starting the week of 20 October? The answer was provided by someone from purchasing. That was the first week that a cheaper grade of CDX plywood was used as a means of cutting costs.

Lessons Learned

The point-persons can be from different organizations as well as different departments. What is key is that they have the mandate from their management to develop standards of method, performance, and behavior. In this case, the point-persons brought in workers to ensure that standards existed from the start. They did not leave this to chance.

Once it had been demonstrated that the standards were in place and were being followed, without hesitation the point-persons began to consider how to make a breakthrough to achieve the goal of the process. This is where the PDSA cycle becomes so effective as a model for improvement. The tools outlined here can help to make breakthroughs if used correctly.

Chapter 16

Notes

Chapter 17

> *Do not lag in zeal,*
> *be ardent in spirit.*
> **Romans 12:11**

A Personal Mission

You may have wondered why I chose the two case studies which were presented in Chapters 7 and 8. In the case of **Making Time for Quality** in the Invoicing Department, although Linda was able to find time for strategic thinking, Christie resigned to find a job which was more suited to her personality. When the vice president directed Dick to empower his sales managers, Dick ended up resigning too. All the remaining case studies exhibited successful applications of the empowerment process.

First, I wanted everyone to realize that empowering workers is a very difficult assignment. It cannot be treated lightly or casually. Any change is disruptive to the activities of an enterprise. **Making Time for Quality** can be extremely stressful because the manager must retain accountability while delegating responsibility. The willing workers on the other hand find it difficult to practice self-discipline even after sufficient training has been provided. Go slowly at first. Get buy-in from everyone involved. This is the purpose of the Contractual Phase.

Second, I want the reader to see both the negatives as well as the positives of **Making Time for Quality.** Anyone can relate success stories. I have tried to paint a more accurate picture of how events could go. So, don't let the first two case studies discourage you from following the process. Christie should have chosen another line of work. Dick's boss handled the **Making Time for Quality** process in the wrong way. Now that you know the pitfalls your chances of success are almost one hundred percent.

Third, four factors impact the success of any organizational change, viz. Change is a function of:

- **D**issatisfaction
- **K**nowledge
- **L**eadership
- **F**ear of Failure.

Without dissatisfaction with the status quo, there will be no change. Without knowledge of a better way to improve the status quo, there will be no change. Without leaders to guide the organization through the transformation, no change will occur. If fear of failure is rampant in the organization, no change will occur. **Making Time for Quality** provides the knowledge factor in the change equation.

$$C = \frac{D \cdot K \cdot L}{F}$$

Management must be dissatisfied, must provide the leadership, and must eliminate the fear of failure before change will occur.

So what is so wonderful about **Making Time for Quality?** It is like regaining control of your life. You will have a chance to get out of the reactionary mode and spend more of your time using Shewhart's Plan-Do-Study-Act cycle in the predictive mode. Continual improvement will become a way of life for you and those who report to you. You and everyone else will have begun to experience quality in your daily work.

Picture yourself standing on the end of a high diving board. You are ready to use the springboard to propel yourself into a beautiful, graceful series of spins, twists, and rolls before a perfect entry into the water. You are apprehensive, maybe even a bit frightened. However, **Making Time for Quality**, is your personal mission. You understand the theory. You know about the dangers. So, go for it!

Chapter 17

Notes

References

1. *The New Economics,* W. E. Deming, 1993 MIT CAES p. 50
2. *The New Economics,* p. 160
3. *Webster's Ninth New Collegiate Dictionary,* p. 408
4. *Out of the Crisis,* W. E. Deming, MIT CAES 1986, p. 276
5. *The Empowered Manager,* Peter Block, Jossey- Bass 1988 p. xvi
6. *Out of the Crisis,* p. 2, 3
7. *Out of the Crisis,* p. 202
8. *Principle Centered Leadership,* Stephen R. Covey, Summit Books, 1990, p. 216
9. Private communication at the PMI seminar, 1988
10. *Process Quality Management & Improvement Guidelines,* AT&T Bell Laboratories, 1987, p. 78
11. Private Conversation with Henry Peters.
12. *Process Control,* Ellis Ott, McGraw Hill, 1974
13. *Out of the Crisis,* p. 276
14. *Out of the Crisis,* p. 237
15. *Out of the Crisis,* p. 357
16. *Continuous Improvement,* Noriaki Kano and Paul Lillrank, Center for Japanese Studies, The University of Michigan, 1989
17. *Out of the Crisis,* Chapter 11
18. *Continuous Improvement*
19. *Improving Quality Through Planned Experimentation,* R.D. Moen, T.W. Nolan, L.P. Provost, McGraw Hill, 1991
20. *"Using New Concepts in the Management of Change in a Technical Organization,"* by Robert J. Wolf, 1967